616.86 W777a 2012
Winship, Gary
Addictive personalities and
why people take drugs : the
spike and the moon

ADDICTIVE PERSONALITIES AND WHY PEOPLE TAKE DRUGS

D0781884

Other titles in the UKCP Series:

ADDICTIVE PERSONALITIES AND WHY PEOPLE TAKE DRUGS
The Spike and the Moon

Gary Winship

On behalf of the
United Kingdom Council for Psychotherapy

KARNAC

CUYAHOGA COMMUNITY COLLEGE
METROPOLITAN CAMPUS LIBRARY

First published in 2012 by
Karnac Books Ltd
118 Finchley Road
London NW3 5HT

Copyright © 2012 by Gary Winship

The right of Gary Winship to be identified as the author of this work have been asserted in accordance with §§ 77 and 78 of the Copyright Design and Patents Act 1988.

All rights reserved. No part of this publication may be reproduced, stored in a retrieval system, or transmitted, in any form or by any means, electronic, mechanical, photocopying, recording, or otherwise, without the prior written permission of the publisher.

British Library Cataloguing in Publication Data

A C.I.P. for this book is available from the British Library

ISBN-13: 978-1-85575-797-4

Typeset by Vikatan Publishing Solutions (P) Ltd., Chennai, India

www.karnacbooks.com

CONTENTS

ACKNOWLEDGEMENTS

I would like to especially acknowledge Brian Woollatt and other colleagues from the Bethlem and Maudsley drug unit: Fiona Firmin, Gwen Sobers, Nobby Clarke, Christine Beecroft, Ben Benjamin, Marianne Cunningham, John Strang, Mike Gossop, and Mike Farrell. Sue Ritter, Joy Bray, Joan Smith, Beatrice Stevens, Jonathon Pedder, and Murray Jackson were my teachers and mentors during my fourteen years at the Maudsley. Bob Hinshelwood, Mike Rustin, and Barry Richards taught me a great deal about research. Critical friends and colleagues have read and commented on various chapters and ideas along the way: Shelley MacDonald, Andy Dominy, Rex Haigh, Sally Hardy, Malcolm Pines, Henri Rey, David Kennard, Paul Williams, Bob Young, Gwen Adshead, Barbara Richards, Davey Rawlinson, Christine English, and Martin Weegman. Anton Obholzer provided helpful feedback on earlier drafts of the book as did Stephen Kemmis. Other colleagues to whom I acknowledge a significant debt for my learning along the way are Dave Foreshaw, Ellen Brown, Cheryl Kipping, Mike Smee, Chris Hart, David Russell, Ben Thomas, Janis Bell, Kris Dominy, Clare Unwin, Simon Burling, Sarah Robson, Peter Helps, Ian Darn, Ishobel Lennox, and Jane Courtney. I am grateful to Emma Cameron and Julia Cameron for reading chapter six and allowing me to write about their sister and reproduce a section of Lucy Cameron's poem, *The Space*. Finally, I acknowledge the many clients who have taught me much along the way.

ABOUT THE AUTHOR

Dr Gary Winship (PhD, MA, RMN, Dip Gp Psych, Cert Add) is a UKCP psychotherapist (UPCA), NMC MHN registered; associate professor, School of Education, University of Nottingham; and senior fellow, Institute for Mental Health, UoN. He has worked with drug users since 1980. He was formerly inpatient unit ward manager and full-time clinical researcher on the Bethlem and Maudsley Hospital drug dependency unit, developing and evaluating health education and harm minimization intervention. With Janis Bell, he co-authored the service protocols for the first dedicated methadone outpatient service in the UK. He is an advocate and supporter of the work of East-West Detox, the UK-based organization that arranges for addicts to go to the Thamkrabok treatment centre in Thailand. He acted as a policy advisor and researcher to the Labour Party, 1992–1994, and Conservative Party, 2006.

Gary Winship was formerly a lecturer at University of Sheffield and University of Reading; visiting lecturer, UCL, University of Greenwich, University of East London, and Goldsmiths College; and senior adult psychotherapist, Berkshire NHS Trust, Broadmoor and Maudsley hospitals. He is a full member of the Association of Psychoanalytic Psychotherapy in the NHS (APP).

PREFACE

On writing off drugs

Is there an overarching explanatory framework for the compulsion and obsession that lies at the heart of the urge to take drugs? Can we talk about an addiction *Weltanschauung*? In order to get to the heart of the common psychological substrate of obsession and addiction I have begun here by returning to some well-known myths. Myths are helpful markers of universal experience. We often see the same stories told with different protagonists, suggesting to us that the narratives are more primary than the characters; the signifiers are less important than what is being signified. Beginning with Dionysus, Shiva, and Prometheus, through to more recent tales of obsession like *Dracula*, I start to carve out a frame for conceptualizing addictive psychology and the layers of motivation behind the compulsion to use drugs. Myths hold great truths, especially where they have lingered. Claude Lévi-Strauss said that trying to read a myth can be a bit like reading sheet music for the untrained eye; at first there appears to be a whole range of peculiar signs dotted about all over the place that seem to have little order or connection. But after a while you begin to see there are patterns emerging.

Signs begin to indicate universals of experience, and it is from here that we start to make sense of what otherwise appeared incomprehensible.

I begin by scoping out the territory of drug addiction today, reviewing the failure of health education and harm minimization. I revisit Herbert Marcuse's (1968) assertion that drugs might fuel the senses for a progressive social revolution. Today, Marcuse's idealism sounds little more than fanciful. But I am not inclined to demonize drugs. Instead, I suggest a new direction where a model of consciousness-raising, rather than aversion, is advanced as an underpinning philosophy for preventing and treating drug misuse in the new millennium. In connecting psychological features of addiction and compulsion I develop a theory about psychotic fixation points, arguably as relevant to working with obsessive compulsive disorders (OCD) and other addictive conditions as much as drug addiction.

To understand the depth of the psychosocial urge to use mind-altering substances, Freud's conundrum about the discontentment of civilization and his assertion that drugs are one of the two great evils, I take as the start point for interrogating the rampant culture of addiction in society today, and the pill mentality that seems to underscore our approach to distress and depression. A fascination with mind-altered states is shown to run through the narrative of many ancient myths. From the creation myth of the Hindu goddess Shiva who made the universe while chewing hashish, to the legendary palace of Xanadu, a number of creation myths are considered where mind-altering substances co-occur. Drawing on the writings of Coleridge, Cocteau, and Burroughs, the essence of a primitive hunger is explored in relation to clinical challenge. The implications of comprehending the essence of deep drug hunger are reviewed in with regard to treatment imperatives.

In the chapter on *Dracula*, Stoker's classic novel about compulsion, I begin with a puzzle posed by a young cocaine user called Arthur: "Why are so many addicts interested in Count Dracula?" Stoker's *Dracula* is found to be an illuminating account of the nature of compulsion. Biographical detail of Stoker and his circle is bringing to light some striking possibilities that the novel is derived from more than a passing interest in the effects of morphine. In placing the count on the couch, hypotheses about a universal fascination with all things vampire is considered. Karl Abraham's observations about the phase of growing teeth, from milk teeth onwards, allows us to develop some specific hypotheses about oral fixation, pain, and drug use. A theory about Scoptophilia and narcissistic wounding frame the aetiology of Dracula's psychopathology. Finally, we return to Arthur's progress, and answer his question about the fascination with Dracula.

The theme of "living death", as in Dracula's case, is further considered in the next chapter where I try to elaborate the Prometheus syndrome. Drug addiction is characterized by repeated acts of masochism and this dynamic is compared to the repetitive attacks on the liver in the myth of Prometheus. Given that drug misuse often leads to liver damage, the plight of Prometheus is shown to be apposite. The often unconscious sadistic self-attacks in drug misuse are considered in relation to the process of psychotherapeutic treatment. Through the course of exploratory talking therapy, self-annihilation tendencies become apparent in the memories, dreams, and imaginings of the patient. The destructive forces at play can be said to be exerting "unconscious" disturbance and it is through tapping into these unconscious dynamics that the addictive urge can be understood. The potential for alteration of the patient's unconscious is explored and the possibility of alleviation of addiction is described. In the process of therapy, the therapist acts as a detoxifying agent for toxic mentations, in a way not dissimilar to the agency of the liver in detoxifying blood.

The self-destructive cycle of death and repair, a repetition-compulsion that seems to have an allure, is a sort of object fascinated death throe that takes us back to Freud's Nirvana Principle. Dionysus guides us through the dangerous potential of wild hedonism and leads us towards a new theory that I call the "pleasure-paradox". The unexpected finding that patients in psychotherapy will give up smoking even when smoking is not a presenting issue, is taken as a basis to reflect on what it is that addicts might need to talk about in the process of treatment. It is argued that talking about drugs, like talking about dieting, can become a compulsion in its own right. In critiquing clinical approaches that place drugs at the centre of focus, it is argued that many approaches to preventing and treating drug addiction adopt an alarmist or aversion inclined approach. A more circumspect analysis is situated in understanding the culture of drug use in modern society. Chronic drug use is a slow death where the self becomes inward-folded and the body becomes a hollow shell of premature decay. The will to pleasure in dangerous drug use seems to be enhanced rather than countered by the drive towards destructiveness. The dichotomy suggests that the oppositional drives of life and death (connoted sometimes as

Eros and Thanatos respectively) push and pull in different directions. For drug users there appears to be a palpable tension inherent in their misuse; as if from the threshold of death there is a peak of life experience. Clinical experience demonstrates that dependency on dangerous activities can be replaced by attachment to persons. The process of the realignment of dependency from pathological to benign dependency is described using case accounts.

Finally, in a chapter that has the rather wordy title of "Major Tom, Lucy, Bion, and the Psychotic Vacuum", I present a triptych of cases which bind together a new frame for understanding the relationship vacuum that is rent from life on drugs. Beginning with a case anecdote about an amphetamine user who was troubled with an underlying psychotic condition, much taken with David Bowie's song *Space Oddity* as a description of his experience of tripping, I try to draw attention to the emptiness in which the client's social relations were conducted. Bion's thoughts on the challenge of linking drug addiction and psychosis are refracted in his personal copy of Rosenfeld's (1965) book *Psychotic States*, where Bion made copious notes in the margins. Some of these notes throw new light on Bion's approach to psychotic fixation, repetition-compulsion, and his understanding of the problem of substance misuse, and attention is drawn particularly to one of Bion's clients whose peculiar ritual in analysis appeared to create a "psychotic space". In the final case presentation the life and death of Lucy Cameron prompts cause for reflection. Lucy's poem *The Space* draws attention to the devastating psychotic vacuum created by substance misuse.

The invocation of some well-known mythologies offers us a starting point to understand addiction and compulsion reaching out across the ages, and across cultural divides. In a world dominated by discontinuities, myths point to the commonality of suffering. In a significant way then, it is literature that offers one steer for the whole of this book. But writing on drugs can be problematic: there is the danger of sensationalism, alarmism, or glamorization. What attracts interest more often than not is the case where the chemical or herbal muse has supposedly invoked some luxuriant lyric, or a vision as Coleridge claimed with *Kubla Khan*, or where the riddles of the future have been imagined as in a speeding Philip K. Dick's *Do Androids Dream of Electric Sheep?* Tales about famous drug users whet our curiosity: Lewis Carroll's rendezvous with mushrooms in writing *Alice in Wonderland* or Robert Louis

Stevenson's meteoric output on mescaline in producing the 60,000 words of *The Strange Case of Dr Jekyll and Mr Hyde* in only six days, or Charles Baudelaire's hypnogogic poetry on hashish. After this we might summon up the writings of Cocteau and Burroughs before we reach the phenomenon of modernity where writers, musicians, and composers, have invoked the chemical muse as an integral component of their creative careers. Indeed, drugs have been a key fuel in the recentindustry of rock and pop.

It would be important to say that not all drug use is pathological: it can be recreational and even normalizing. For some young people, taking hallucinogens can be normalizing and part of a transition from adolescence to adulthood (Macdonald et al., 1997). And taking drugs has, on occasions, been described as a route to opening the psychic doors to a higher plane of consciousness (Marcuse, 1968; Leary, 1970). Even if the answer to the universe is lost upon waking from the drug sleep cycle, the boundless allure of searching for the answer remains. It would be mundane to consider all the would-be writers who, having ingested their substance of choice, having then spent the next several hours fixed to the spot staring at a snag of carpet, re-emerging later with little more than a blank repose and an empty mind. The enticement of drugs for the literati is plain, and the output stokes a referential cycle which becomes the yoke of curiosity for each new generation.

Our interest coalescing around "celebrated" writers, including more lately artists and musicians, runs a course that skirts tragedy and genius in close measure, Amy Winehouse perhaps being the best known recent example. But even where there is the apparent success of writing on drugs, there is always the question as to whether it has anything to do with the drug at all, as Sadie Plant (1999) ultimately inquires. There is a suspicion, for instance, that Coleridge rather fabricated the idea of his drug-induced vision in *Kubla Khan* and that the time lapse between its reputed frantic composition and its final publication several years later suggests that the success of the poem owed more to Coleridge's skills in redrafting than the so-called genius of his laudanum muse. Where there has been the glimmer of an inspirational yield from drugs, I am yet to be convinced that it has had anything to do with drug use anyway. That is not to say that Stevenson's stamina for his six-day composition might not be credited to the wakening sustenance provided by his intake of mescaline, nor can Jack Kerouac's (1958) three-day blitz to produce *The Subterraneans* be said to have nothing to do with the ingestion of a large amount of benzedrine. However, in each of these cases, it must be the talent of the writer that wins through the hazy muse of the potion.

If I do not subscribe to the idea that drugs somehow open the doors of perception then it would seem I begin by a nullifying reduction; as if I am writing off drugs. Drugs are a favourite pastime of many, including the rich and famous, and the use of drugs does not always lead to addiction. So it might seem churlish on my part to have such a downer on drugs. However, in ethical deference to the struggles of most of the addicts I have worked with over the years, their drug mis-use has so weighed them down that they have been miles from any aesthetics of higher drug-induced perception. My client Spike was your average drug user. He was called Spike by his mates, because there was a collapse between his identity and the needles that had turned his body into an infected pin-cushion. Like so many other people I have worked with, Spike's drug use had crushed him. He was closer to annihilation than liberation. In Chapter Four I talk about how Spike's self annihilation rippled across the lives of many others. His story presses home how the suffering of one person can impact on the lives of many.

My clinical concerns have rarely traversed to a study of what people do on drugs; rather I have been interested to know what people are like when they are not using drugs. In a way then, this book is more about people off drugs, than about writing on drugs. You might even say that this book has nothing to do with drugs, but were I to borrow Winnicott's aphorism of no-such-thing-as-baby, I might lay claim to there being no such thing as a drug problem. There are, of course, only problem drug users. My interest lies in what clients are like once they have ceased using drugs or what they were like *before* they were using drugs in the first place. It might seem a more sombre project, a bit like throwing cold water on the glamour of chemically raised conscious-ness. But I think it is worth announcing here the intention is to evoke self-reflection on a predicament; that it is tragedy not glamour that courses through modern life. The backbone of the thesis here is that we are a culture obsessed, obsessed by domination, failure, celebrity, and sex, and that this "culture of compulsion" is epitomized by the allure of drugs, both prescribed and non-prescribed. I do want to single out for particular attention the current dominant paradigm of the approach to drug addiction in the UK which clusters around the idea of health education and harm minimization. In spite of the monies poured into health education strategies since the 1980s the massive increase in the number of drug users indicates a deep failure of philosophy.

There are others who have seen drugs in a different light, and some who I profoundly admire. The idea that drugs might have revolutionary potential interested Herbert Marcuse (1968). He became the hero and spokesman for the student generation in the 1960s when he asserted that drugs would prime the awareness of the need for revolution: "the kernel of truth in the psychedelic search" (1968, p. 44) he called it. He was not the first. The Surrealists experimented with a modified version of the psychoanalytic technique of free association in producing words and pictures using the ingestion of caffeine to prick them awake to produce semi-conscious writings: the technique of "hypnotic slumber" involving simultaneous composition with dream activity. In 1920 Breton and his fellow poet Phillipe Soupault honed their free flow technique of "automatic writing", producing the first surrealist text, *Magnetic Fields* (1920). What would a utopian like Marcuse now say about the aftermath of the drug revolution? Would he say social progress would have been better served in a sane society rather than a psychedelic one? When Leary (1970) reported that hallucinogens had given him the "most deeply religious experience" of his life, I do indeed grasp that he experienced an illusion so powerful that it might be compared to religion. Drugs can serve to create an illusion, and it is strange that we have come to have reverence for a temporary psychosis. This proves no more progressive than any prior religious illusion, and perhaps we might add that drugs have been a stunting phenomena deepening the pitiful ontological sleep of the polity. Herewith I take a lead from Freud's announcement that drugs and religion are the two worst evils of civilization and its discontents.

In their writings on drugs Marcuse and Leary should be assigned their place as part of a generation of prophets seeking whimsical direction after the fall. The idea that drugs would liberate society sounds now little more than a fanciful lyric. Drugs and liberation folded back in on themselves, and after the flower there was no power, only collapse. The "pill mentality", as we saw it emerge since the 1950s became a chemical tsunami by the end of the millennium. Can we envisage another vista, one where mass drug retreat is replaced by a new civil alertness? We do not have to subscribe to an age of parsimonious civil obedience and psychic sanitization, rather a social order where agitation and conflict can rouse the passion of sober anarchy that might project us towards a better society. It may be the revolutionary potential of sobriety which transforms the status quo. The numbing effects of mass drug use serve well to induce malaise, solidifying the stagnating forces of democracy. The opium of the masses has become just that.

In spite of the unprecedented human capital invested in combating the problem of drug misuse since the late 1970s, the scale of the drug problem in the UK and the West has continued to escalate. It is fair to say that addiction is nothing short of being a public health disaster, that impacts on as many lives as other major pandemics like cholera or typhoid. Over the last three decades, resources have been directed towards harm minimization and maintenance strategies which have sought to ensure that addicts use their drugs safely. Not only have these strategies failed to halt the spiral of drug misuse, there are grounds to wonder whether the drug epidemic has been a by-product of health education and harm reduction models. The costs of prescribing treatments have escalated, and even more so with the prescribing of buprenorphine which, since its launch in 1999, has rapidly become seen as an alternative to methadone treatment in the United Kingdom, accounting for 45% of opiate prescription costs in England (based on prescription figures for 28 Strategic Health Authorities (SHAs) in England 2001–2003). Adding to the already expensive prescription of methadone, there is nonetheless scant evidence about buprenorphine's effectiveness (de Wet et al., 2005).

Government's continuing willingness to invest in interventions is probably to be applauded. In a national treatment outcomes study (NTORS), treatment costs for 549 clients, recruited from addiction programmes both in the community and residential settings, were calculated to be £2.9 million in the two years prior to index treatment, and a further £4.4 million in the subsequent two years (Godfrey et al., 2004). However, the government relies on the advice of experts as to how this money should be invested, and it would seem that, for the most part at least, effective services have *not* been funded. After an extended review of the literature on the effectiveness of treatment, prevention, and enforcement in the USA (Reuter & Pollack, 2006), it was concluded that there was very little evidence that even relatively well-funded treatment systems were reducing the number of people in a nation who engaged in problematic drug use. In terms of law enforcement, research has failed almost uniformly to show that intensified policing or sanctions have reduced either drug prevalence or drug-related harm.

It is timely to re-appraise how we approach the problem of addiction. This book marks out a new direction, not only in offering clinicians new theoretical frameworks for working with addicts, but also in transforming general attitudes to the way in which drugs are perceived in society today. *The Spike and the Moon* begins with the task of how to engage with drug users in therapeutic conversations and follows through various stages of recovery, mapping the emotional, social, and psychological pathways to the cessation of addiction. Crucially, the inclination to the over-interventionism of models of health education is taken to task. The dominance of what we might think of as an "aversion approach" to therapeutic intervention, especially with drug education in schools, is turned on its head and superseded by a framework of consciousness-raising. Engaging with drug users about the dangers of their drug use, talking to them about how it is likely to harm them, may well appeal to the addict's appetite for the alluring brinkmanship of life and death. The health warning on cigarette packets, "Smoking kills", may paradoxically be the best advertising a tobacco company could desire. We have a health industry that serves to keep the drug of interest at the centre of attention.

Addicts have been sold short because fewer and fewer people have taken the time to wonder why they take drugs, let alone how they might stop. *The Spike and the Moon* is based on an extensive investigation into the patterns of attachment among addicted persons. It draws attention to dynamic commonalities, continuities, and discontinuities in formative relationships and then relationships in recovery. As these patterns come into focus, it has been possible to throw new light on not only the developmental course of addiction, but also what might be indicated in terms of treatment intervention. The findings confirm a core condition that treatment interventions should focus primarily on relationships, both from the perspective of aetiology and then later as a basis for recovery.

Confluence

In setting out a context for this I would like to emphasize the fact that the theories unfolded here are not isolated to drug users alone. One of the problems of addiction theory is that it can be ghettoized, somehow cut off from other psychological theories. The subtitle for the book refers to the psychology of obsession, and I am sure that the idea of the Prometheus Syndrome (which is unfolded in Chapter Four) is, for instance, equally applicable to other self-destructive patterns of behaviour such as self harm.

And we know that psychotic states are characterized by a ruminating and fixed system of beliefs. These beliefs can be so fixed and unshifting that they become chronic conditions, like a psychotic vacuum, a feeling of an empty dark space that eats up all the goodness if your life. The addictive urge can be very single minded, and might be compared to the delusion system in psychosis which is impressively enduring were it not so damaging. It is a concentration of attention on delusions and recurring hallucinations which means other beliefs can be suspended. I am not so convinced by the idea of schizoid splitting as Klein (1946) calls it, nor Bion's idea of psychotic and non-psychotic aspects of the personality. It seems to me that a psychotic state is altogether more tangled. The patterns of repetition apparent in drug addiction and the idea of *psychotic vacuum* might be a useful way of thinking about these mental processes. In the same way that we refer to a drug fix, we might think also of a psychotic fix. The therapist's role is to act as a ground control to clients cut adrift and floating in a psychotic space. The challenge for the therapist is to act as a detoxifying agent, to access the destructivity and toxic object relations and help the client replace these with a new synthesis of tonic relations.

Where I have had occasion to couch ideas in terms of a psychological theory of addiction, on occasions I have opted to follow the course of what is best described as "object relations theory" (ORT). I think it is fair to say that ORT is a more rudimentary idea in depth psychology than might otherwise first appear; it is more easily grasped than many uninitiated might think. I do not concur with the late Stephen Mitchell (1994) that ORT is in danger of becoming too popular, threatening to degenerate into a tired psychoanalytic cliché. If there is a danger, it is that object relations theory has not thinned enough into clinical maxims that have easily managed to transcend popular therapeutic discourses. The value of a psychoanalytic theory has, since Freud, been measured in its ability to exert value for every mental health practitioner among psychiatrists, nurses, counsellors, social workers, psychologists, teachers, and so on. The ideas of transference, or attachment theory for instance, have shown themselves to be indispensable to many cross-disciplinary practitioners. The same cannot be said of some other useful ORT ideas such as projective identification, splitting, containment, and so on. That is a shame.

I believe ORT is a helpful berth for the foregoing study of addiction and compulsion. In following the progress of developmental psychology and social psychology in the twentieth century, ORT has held with the notion that external (other) experiences are primarily more influential than the bubbling cauldron of instinctual drives that emerge from within. ORT offers a route to an outside-in way of thinking, countering the predominance of inside-out theories that posit selfwill, genetics, or biological imbalance as the causal root of addictive disorders. ORT offers a modern trajectory for philosophical custom,; a subject-object differentiation that sits closer to Husserl than Kant, but necessarily derives from both. It may seem strange that the term "object" is used to refer to people or "parts" of people, like the breast, the eye, and so forth: a kind of ORT chopped-up *Frankenstein* of language. But in addiction the various parts of the body are abused: veins, skin, nose, internal body parts too, for example the liver, kidney, or heart, or the lungs of the smoker. The damage may be concentrated, but it might annihilate the whole (as I discuss in Chapter Six). ORT allows us to simultaneously talk about mental and psychological processes while holding in mind the organic influence of flesh, blood, and body parts so to speak.

There is no doubt in my mind that problem drug use emerges from in-depth problems of one sort or another. And so it is towards these depths that this book bends: the lower regions, the nightmare of the underworld. As the opening inscription of Freud's (1900) *The Interpretation of Dreams* puts it: *acheronta si movebo*—"If I cannot move to the higher powers I will bend to the lower regions." Freud's inscription in his dream book was taken from Virgil: Dante's guide through hell, so we assume Freud meant for psychoanalysis to be at home in hell. Psychoanalysis is always one lens of refraction as a paradigm response to despair. In identifying some dark mythical figures as guides in this study, I follow a conviction that it is in the twilight land of dreams and imaginings that a path forward might emerge. As Dante did, we must wander from the path if we are to see the world as it really is, with all its pain, hypocrisy, corruption, and injustice. Only when we have contemplated the depths can we resurface with hope anew.

But do we "abandon all hope" when entering the underworld of addiction? Maybe. Working with addicts can get to you, it gets under your skin. It can become a kind of psychic septicaemia if you do not get detoxified regularly enough. I have been struck by the way in which some images can become lodged like a psychic Polaroid, haunting freeze-frames of dirty needles, children playing hopscotch over bloody barrels near flats off the Walworth Road, parents drunk unconscious in the outpatient clinic while their baby screams blue murder, patients oblivious to HIV vowing to trust their partner with their life, only to discover that they have. The working through of the trauma is the basis of recovery; in Narcotics Anonymous they call it "sharing"; the more we hear the stories of others the more we learn about ourselves. Part of this book emerges from trauma, and in part the aim is to share to see if this might help others. I hope so.

A note on research

I want at this point to make one last note about the cycle of research that sits at the heart of this book. Counsellors and psychotherapists often appear to lack the will to articulate the strength of reflective research that underpins their clinical practice. But, the academic necessity of positioning a methodology that lays claim to empirical rigour, and therefore validity of assertions, is needed. Michael Rustin's (2001) work on the generation of knowledge in psychotherapy refers us to the way in which small case study methods can generate a critical mass of data when practitioners compare their case by case findings with those of their colleagues. In other words, through the process of reflecting on case practice, either in supervision or later by publishing findings, single case study data can accumulate into more generalizable assertions about efficacy. Rustin argues that psychotherapy practice might even be considered as an exemplar of research consistency where the consulting room can act as a controlled space for observing case by case differentials, and thereafter any clinical change in clients. If clinicians conduct their work within the framework of similar operational patterns, that is to say, same room, same time, consistent use of technique, and so on, the approach then starts to resemble a laboratory type of research. Single case narratives can be illuminating and persuasive in ways that quantitative studies cannot impact on the field of mental health. Take for instance the cases of Victoria Climbié or Baby Peter, both single case inquiries which have had a profound impact on policy and professional practice (Winship, 2007). We should never doubt the persuasiveness of qualitative case study data in reaching beyond the scope of large numbers.

I also want to note the international scope of the ideas in this book. In order to overhaul assumptions about addiction and its treatment, *The Spike and the Moon* returns to the problem of "Why do people take drugs?" The central argument here is that addiction is not only ingrained in individual personalities, but also imprinted in culture. So there must be a question as to whether cultures of drug use are different across nation states? What we do know is that drug abuse exists across the world; it is one of the unifying contingencies of human suffering. Like any pandemic, the health consequences of illicit substance misuse stretch far and wide. The debate about the so-called "war on drugs" seems to offer a rubric that draws attention to the international weave of the drug misuse pandemic. Opium produced by the peasants in Afghanistan or cannabis cultivated in northern Africa can wend its way into the hearts and lungs of kids on the streets in any number of towns and cities around the world. The suffering caused by drug misuse knits us globally together we might say.

Then further down in the social system there are local drug geographies to consider. A group of adolescents sniffing glue in a small town in Cornwall may have a different constituency to a group of young people sniffing glue in Haringey in London. But there may also be some core psychological contingencies that transcend international and local geographies. Can the habitual use of heroin by a young addict in Thailand resemble that of the addiction to heroin of a young man somewhere in Europe? To some extent the answer is yes. There are at least two case vignettes in this book based on my work with two young Muslim addicts where it appears that the urge towards using illicit drugs as a psychic retreat is little different to the type of addictive urges you might see in any young white British drug user. In other words there appear to be psychological commonalties of addiction, and its aetiology, that transcend cultural, social, religious, and political divides. There are some universals after all, like the moon. It is the same moon, no matter where you are.

CHAPTER ONE

Fixing the pill mentality

From Freud to flower power

In response to the UK government's *Drug Strategy Unit Report* (DSU, 2005) *The Guardian* newspaper (July 6, 2005) front page led with the headline, "How the war on drugs has failed". The DSU report estimated that there were three million illicit substance users and that 56 per cent of all crimes were drug related with the cost of drug associated crimes rising to 16 billion pounds, then upwards of 24 billion when health and social care expenses were added in.

Drug use in the UK has reached such a level that it has become nothing short of a public health disaster, and an exceedingly expensive one at that. But the tragedy is far more than an economic one. A report from the National Programme on Substance Abuse Deaths (2008) led by St George's, University of London, drew attention to the fact that drug-related deaths have continued to steadily rise in the UK, despite our best efforts over the last thirty years to curb the worst effects of substance misuse. In the economic analysis of the "war on drugs", there is some agreement that drugs will be imported as long as the market exists. In other words it is the appetite for drugs that dictates the market, not the strategies of Customs & Excise control.

And yet strategies that might address the underpinning appetite for drugs have been conspicuous in their absence. Instead, the worst effects of the illicit drug market have been met with interventions clustering around the philosophy of harm minimization, replacement prescribing either for oral or injecting use, methadone maintenance programmes, needle exchange schemes, and so on. The philosophy of health education and harm minimization has the hue of a defeated paradigm, as if we cannot help people to stop taking drugs, so we may as well teach people how to take drugs safely. Harm minimization has become a system of circular interventions that has seen drug users persuaded away from the illicit drug market by the offer of more drugs. In other words, what we have is a system where it is accepted wisdom to treat someone's drug problem by giving them another drug. In time we may look back at our chemical era with some chagrin.

The prescribing glut that began in the 1960s has gathered pace ever since. The rise of pharmaceuticals and psychiatric medication is especially complicit, driven by the chimera of chemical solutions for society's ills. There can be no eschewing the dominance of a medical hegemony which has fuelled the appetite for drugs, both illicit and legal drugs. We have come to live in what might be called a pill mentality culture. Psychiatry has been the new church for "chemical ceremonials" says Szasz, T. (1974), where the search for the panacea of short-cut pharmaceutical solutions has driven the largest amount of research into the field of mental health (Winship & Hardy, 2007). There have been attempts to rein in the amount of prescribing: for instance in the 1990s there was a concerted effort to curtail the over-prescribing of valium and other anxiolytics which were shown to be highly addictive. In 2006, Dr Colin Brewer, an internationally renowned expert in addiction was found guilty by the General Medical Council of irresponsibly handing out large quantities of drugs without assessing the needs of his patients. There have been other occasional outcries, for instance a more recent strong reaction to the over-prescribing of drugs for a number of childhood disorders. But these voices are generally drowned out by the noise of the juggernaut that is the pharmaceutical industry.

The profile of the workforce of practitioners who encounter drug users has seen an ever-increasing number of professionals trained in *sustaining* drug intake. HIV and AIDS prompted big changes in attitude towards safe drug use from the 1980s onwards, particularly concerned with attempting to prevent users from sharing or engaging in other risky activities where the HIV might be spread, such as unsafe sex. However, studies of sharing among injecting drug users has highlighted that in spite of the first two decades of health promotion, between 78 per cent to 94 per cent of drug users were still sharing equipment (Bennett et al., 2000; Hunter et al., 2000). Indeed, there may be some evidence here that our attempts at health education, such as needle exchange schemes and replacement prescribing, have made the situation worse. Substance misuse has become the type of an iatrogenic problem that Illich (1976) has so cogently described.

So what is to be done? In the second half of this chapter I am going to propose a theory about the "fix" we are in when it comes to meeting the challenge of drug addiction and substance misuse. My thesis rests on the idea that the systems and paradigms of treatment we have evolved over the last thirty years are in some way part of the madness. The system is mad because it unthinkingly repeats the same self-defeating cycle of repetition-compulsion that is the problem itself, in other words the treatment paradigm of harm minimization and health education simply mirrors and perpetuates the substance misuse rather than reshaping and challenging it. Much of this unthinkingness is unconscious, so we need to raise consciousness about the human nature of substance misuse. It will always be timely to re-think our attitudes towards drugs and treatment, and perhaps more so in times of economic recession. Addiction in an age of austerity might change the goal posts. We cannot afford to go on in the same way that we have been.

Addicts have been sold short because fewer and fewer people have been interested in helping them understand why they need to take drugs and how they might be helped to stop. When someone stops taking drugs, and more importantly stays stopped, it is worth discovering why this has happened. It is one of the shortfalls of psychological research today that there are rarely any depth accounts as to why some people achieve sobriety and others do not. A depth psychology perspective might start to throw some light on the motivation behind the appetite for drugs, and provide an account of motivation as well as an indication of what constitutes a successful programme of recovery. But an intensive account of the individual psychology of addiction must stand alongside the co-occurring causal pathways such as poverty, social deprivation, unemployment, social exclusion, lack of education and opportunity, and so on.

The idea that social-pathogens can flank faulty mentalizations provides us with a robust developmental frame for unmasking drug misuse, and this was Freud's (1930) starting point in *Civilization and*

Its Discontents. Freud argued that any research into the private ills of mankind should begin with a dual lens where sociology could frame depth psychology. Freud believed that everyone was faced with the dread of remorseless pressure from the external world, full of suffering, inhibitions, anxieties, and the unavoidable biological truth of bodily deterioration. The urge to retreat from reality was universal and averting suffering and the un-pleasure of life was therefore as fundamental to human nature as breathing, so Freud concluded. He saw that there were several ways in which man could attempt to control the conditions of pleasure and un-pleasure in life. One way was to become isolated like a hermit, to turn away from the anguish of the world. Another was to find religion as a mechanism of defence to mitigate the worst effects of reality by creating an illusion that there was a great overseeing protector. But by far the most effective and powerful defence, Freud concluded, was the chemical one. He noted how intoxication could produce an immediate pleasurable state: "With the help of the 'drowner of cares' one can at any time withdraw from the pressure of reality and take refuge in a world of one's own with better conditions of sensibility" (Freud, 1930, p. 15).

Of course in the end, all these defence manoeuvres would prove ineffective because social isolation, whether it be a religious or chemical retreat into unreality, was antithetical to man's basic gregarious nature. Isolation would lead to deterioration in the organism, so it was a no-win situation, concluded Freud. Man was damned by his civil membership and damned without it. It is of note that while Freud briefly offered an overarching diagnosis about the sociology of drug use, he nonetheless pointed to a cellular explanation of the way in which the mind might otherwise construct countermeasures to defend against reality: "There must be substances in the chemistry of our own bodies which have similar effects [to intoxication], for we know of at least one pathological state, mania, in which a condition similar to intoxication arises without the administration of any intoxicating drug" (1930, p. 15). Freud was looking for an answer in the chemistry of the organism. Perhaps the nearest we have is the existence of natural endorphins which have an opiate-like effect and have been shown to diminish in number when synthesized opiates are ingested. But it would seem that Freud was grasping at straws.

Nonetheless, the formulation of addiction as a psychic retreat from the real world was a persuasive start point. Freud said that this retreat resulted in a great waste of energy which might otherwise be put to better use. He pointed out: "They [drugs] are responsible ... for the useless waste of large quotas of energy which might have been employed for the improvement of the human lot" (1930, p. 15). Freud used *Civilization and Its Discontents* to signpost a method for pursuing intensely focused inquiry into the individual psyche, that is exploratory psychological analysis, while remaining mindful of the prevailing social and civil context of human nature. It was a premise for a type of "clinical sociology", for want of a better term, where the alleviation of compulsive appetites could make the world a better place. At its most ambitious, the revolutionary significance of community sobriety should not be understated and as Freud mused, what if the large quotas of energy wasted on drug use were to be re-channelled? It is not hard to imagine it would be the basis for envisaging an agenda for social revolution, a polity where energy is reinvested for the yield of common wealth and communal well-being.

Such a drug-free Utopia might seem a long way off, considering we are amidst a pandemic of drug misuse which seems set to maintain a steady upward trajectory. Drugs are not the only obsession, however. We are a culture obsessed society: obsessed by celebrity, gadgets, sex, shopping, terror (local and international). We might say this "culture of obsession" is the heir to Lasch's (1977) culture of narcissism, that is to say, the social disposition of self-serving indulgence in the developed world in the mid- to late twentieth century. Lasch considered that there was a social bent towards parasitic relationships where intimacy lacked depth, and general social transactions were characterized by exploitation and irresponsibility. This narcissistic culture saw a general disposition to the procurement of "things" that brought more insularity, albeit with qualification of comfort and pleasure, but nonetheless making lives more inward folded.

> Affluence in the West has seen this reliance on "things", rather than relationships, steadily growing. Technology has meant that domesticity has become more insular, the telephone, the television, the washing machine, and so on. We don't wash laundry in public much anymore (Lasch, 1977).

The procurement of a range of functional devices has seemingly become a necessity and self-sufficiency has been surpassed by techno-social sufficiency. This state of reliance on things is not necessarily pathological, but there is an abundance of disposability when it comes to their use. Marcuse (1964) said that we had evolved a universal one-dimensional social psyche driven by the "overwhelming need for the production and consumption of waste" (p. 7). Perhaps well ahead of his time, Marcuse talked about brands, gadgets, and a consumer culture that stupefied any desire for liberation. And he said that the so-called new modes of "relaxation", like television watching, served mostly to prolong social apathy. Real relationships are replaced with virtual ones, more easily disposable, more autistic than authentic.

Although Marcuse did not refer to drug misuse in *One Dimensional Man*, the emergence of drug use from the 1960s onwards would seem to be a marker for the way in which we have become a dependent consumer obsessed society. Later, in an *Essay of Liberation*, Marcuse (1968) did single out psychedelic drugs for special attention. In response to the widespread use of psychedelics in the late 1960s, Marcuse argued that drugs, or at least hallucinogens, might be the exception to the consumption rule. In other words, rather than subduing the urge for liberation, drugs might be one means to unleashing the revolutionary potential of the psyche, a shift from its one-dimensional obsession into a psychotropic pluralism. Marcuse set himself as a pacifist and a champion of hippie culture where repressive sexual morals could be challenged:

> Obscene is not the woman who exposes her pubic hair but that of a fully clad general who exposes his medals rewarded in a war of aggression; obsession is not the ritual of hippies but the declaration of a high dignitary of the church that war is necessary for peace (1968, p. 18).

He envisaged the opening-up of the popular imagination where new aesthetic dimensions would be a gauge for a free society, where values of creativity, love, and peace could be invoked to overhaul the establishment. Marcuse was taken by the phenomena of drug induced tripping and he referred to use of "pot", "grass", and "acid" (1968, p. 41). The trip, he asserted, might challenge and transform social taboos through new mediums of perception:

> Today's rebels want to see, hear, feel new things in a new way: they link liberation with the dissolution of ordinary and orderly perception. The "trip" involves the dissolution of the ego shaped by established society—an artificial and short-lived dissolution.

But the artificial and private liberation anticipates, in a distorted
manner, an exigency of the social liberation: the revolution must be
at the same time a revolution in perception which will accompany
the material and intellectual reconstruction of society, creating the
new aesthetic environment (1968, pp. 43–44).

Marcuse's vision is at once captivating, but with hindsight it seems to
be little more than a fanciful lyric. What might Marcuse have made of
the collapse of the flower power revolution? One of the slogans of the
punk movement in the late 1970s was "Kill a hippie". The hippie revolution had done little to dent the culture of consumerism that Marcuse
had railed against. Indeed, given that drugs and pharmaceuticals
became one of the most successful industries of capitalism, the flower
power generation turned out to be one of its best customers. We might
say that by the end of the twentieth century the Marxist metaphor for
the religiously subdued spirit of the oppressed, religion as the opium
of the masses, had been replaced by opiates being the opiate of the
masses, a simile of the thing itself.

Far from agitating the collective march towards equality and redis-
tributing wealth among classes, the sum total of the pharmaceutical
industry, and the illicit pharmaceutical industry, became an economic
exemplar of capitalism assigning social deprivation ever more securely
to the lower and under classes. It would be hard for Marcuse to deny
that rather than being the route to liberation, it was substance misuse
and not religion that was at the other side of the barricades. Marcuse's
notion of the new sensorium of drugs priming the awareness of the
need for revolution, "the kernel of truth in the psychedelic search"
(1968, p. 44), became nothing less than the poetry of an idealist. Drugs
and liberation folded back in on themselves; no flower, no power, only
collapse.

By the end of the twentieth century drugs were more the mechanism
of inculcating the indolence of radical potential than the instrument of
emancipation in the good society. To some extent, Lasch's narcissistic
individual had become epitomized in the stereotype of the drug addict:
self-serving and self-obsessed. This stereotype might have taken the
form of the "mythical junkie" so to speak (Gossop, 1982), and may have
served to draw our focus away from the more universal culture of drug
consumption that plagued us: alcohol, psychiatric drugs, and so forth.
But if indeed we had moved from a culture of narcissism to a culture of

compulsive consumption, then the allure of drugs, both prescribed and non-prescribed, has become one of the most modern of appetites. The proliferation of the appetite for drugs which can control emotion, pain, and mood: a pill to pep you up, a pill to bring you down, a pill to stop you eating, a pill to take away the voices, the headache, and the pill to end all pills, the birth control pill.

Madness, repetition-compulsion, and a philosophy for a new Utopia

As I described earlier, my supposition here is that the paradigms of health education and harm minimization in the field of substance misuse treatment, reflect and perpetuate the madness that is the presenting condition. We are dominated by a "pill mentality", in part a cultural illusion that we might somehow fix our mental distress with recourse to mind-altering substances. For the addict this illusion presents as a something that we might call "psychotic fixing", and I will attempt to show that there are core features of repetition-compulsion in addiction and obsessive compulsive disorders that we need to consider if we are to meaningfully get to grips with the reasons why people become addicted. If we can be mindful of the points of psychotic fixation in substance misuse, then perhaps we can start to challenge the pathology and build more robust models of intervention that can facilitate recovery.

A rather enigmatic quote from Wilfred Bion which sets the tone for debate;

> I am the dreamer. I am the den in which I was buried. Who are you?
> I am the thought that found a thinker. Who are you?
> I am the robber who drugged you so you would not know you were being conceptualised. I am the dream that drugged you …

(Bion, 1975, p. 44).

The relationship between the dream and the drug, as Bion suggests, has ancient connotations, the term morphine deriving from Morpheus who in Greek mythology was known as the shaper of dreams, son of Hypnos (god of sleep) and Nyx (goddess of the night). Morpheus is apposite because chronic addiction appears rather like an extended hypnogogic state, a permanent twilight world where real and hallucinated experiences exist in an almost seamless exchange. This twilight world has something of the quality of an "interzone" (Burroughs, 1959), a world between worlds if you like. We might think of this interzone in terms of a collapse between dreaming and waking where the membrane that separates dream work from consciousness is damaged: the dream cannot be contained within sleep because censorship is stolen or inert; sleep is not protected and therefore cannot truly occur. Insomnia might well be characterized by the absence of a capacity for dreaming rather than determined by the absence of sleep. In short, we might say, we drug because we cannot dream.

In order to penetrate this fixed and nightmarish drug dream world the therapist needs to be versed in the way of dreams. In the short fragment above, Bion (1975) compresses the idea of drug use with the process of dreaming linking the dynamic to the most primitive of events: the point of conception itself. Bion suggests that the drug user's capacity to dream has been stolen. Like the schizophrenic patient who, at least in some phases of the illness, is neither asleep nor awake but continually deprived of the capacity to dream, the drug user has lost the capacity to dream. The drug addict exists in a twilight world that comes to resemble a waking recurring nightmare of bizarre sights and objects.

Bion's poetic quote above also has the rhythm of repetition: "I am, I am …". This repetition is noteworthy. We refer to psychosis being a delusional system of repeating fixed beliefs. And these beliefs can be impressively unshifting over many years. The patient who believes that there is a satellite recording his every move is not amenable to rational explanation, cognitive retraining, or pharmaceutical intervention. The delusion will remain a constant, becoming embellished perhaps with other delusions leading to an ever more elaborate network of conspiracy. The delusional system can become frozen into an obsessive re-enactment of actions and behaviours.

For instance Martin had used amphetamines over a number of years until his life was dominated by his appetite for speeding. He reported that at first the fact that he kept seeing a Frenchman on a bicycle carrying onions over his shoulder, was rather amusing to him. Over time it seemed that any sight of a cyclist was transformed into the Frenchman hallucination. At first he knew it was a hallucination. But then he started to hear the French cyclist coming around the corner, even when he could not see him. The absence of a visual cue was a notable sensory change in the intensity of his paranoia as a system of auditory hallucinations began to accompany the optical disturbance. After three or so years of the same hallucinations the idea of the bicycling Frenchman had ceased to be anywhere amusing. He began to feel persecuted and harassed. The bicycling Frenchman was everywhere now. Martin began to arm himself with knives believing that he was being followed by "the onion man". Indeed, anyone arriving at his house, and even people he knew and once was friendly or loving towards, were now scrutinized for their part in the conspiracy led by the Onion Man. Martin's conspiracy theory was a third and final level in the formation of his psychosis where the initial visual hallucination and the subsequent auditory hallucination were embedded in an elaborate psychotic meta-narrative. Martin became socially withdrawn. Even during phases where he managed to cease using drugs, the hallucinations and delusions continued. The police were eventually called after Martin threatened a passer-by outside his house with a knife. The long-term psychological effect of his enduring hallucinatory experience was manifest in severe psychological, social, and physical consequences. He became unemployable and his intimate relationships collapsed. As a result of injecting with dirty needles he developed bacterial endocarditis which was treated with an aortic valve replacement. He successfully completed the initial stages of an inpatient detoxification, but he died a short while later as a result of complications from his valve replacement.

In another case, Sandra, a woman in her mid 30s, reported that for many years while using cocaine, she would become frozen and inert with fear. She would find herself paralyzed, seemingly fixed to the spot, unable to move. Sitting in a chair or lying in a corner, she would harbour the idea that if she moved she would be attacked by a monstrous force. Such was the force of these beliefs, on some occasions she would stay still for so long that she would be incontinent. During the course of psychotherapy we began to understand that these frozen states appeared to be related to her earlier experiences. As a child she had been beaten repeatedly by her father. He would use a wet towel or a belt. On one occasion she said she was beaten so badly that she lost consciousness. She did not recall her mother ever intervening. She later said that her paternal grandfather had committed suicide when her father was four years old. The violence of her childhood was compounded during her adolescence. In her late teens she was raped, but had not been able to tell anyone. She felt guilty, as if it were her fault. She gouged the inside of her womb with a coat hanger believing that she might be pregnant. This had led to gynaecological complications a few years later and the development of pre-cancerous cells which were laser treated. She thought that there was a link between the cancer and the rape, that the cancer was punishment because the rape was her "fault" she said.

I have yet to hear a clear explanation as to why delusional states remain so fixed, either in psychosis or in obsessive compulsive disorders (OCD). Hallucinations remain unmodified, over time becoming fixed in a recurring system of beliefs and these remain strikingly fixed over many years. The delusions and accommodations of behaviour intensify, bringing about a deteriorating level of social functioning, as was the case with Martin and Sandra. There would appear to be connecting features in repeating states of mind, the repeating hallucination of the Onion Man for Martin and the repeating frozen state for Sandra, so how do we understand this in relation to drug use?

With reference to Andrew whose case trajectory is similar to Martin's, I think it is possible to draw some parallels between OCD and compulsive drug misuse. Andrew was a taxi driver who was referred to an NHS outpatient psychotherapy department for treatment of his OCD. Though not a drug user, the emergence of Andrew's fixed delusional system runs a similar course to Martin's. Andrew had developed a belief that he had run someone over. This type of guilty delusion of accidental homicide, in my experience, is more commonplace than one might expect. Andrew's belief was vague in the first place and may have even started in his late teens. When he began driving for a living, there were occasions when something would catch him out of the corner of his eye, or in the side mirror. He would believe he had glimpsed a body lying in the road behind him. These recurring episodic visual hallucinations increased and intensified over a period of several years in his early-mid 20s. Then he became more preoccupied with the anxiety that he was going to run someone over. He was prescribed antidepressants, but these did not help. Eventually he could not even drive a short distance because he would need to keep stopping his vehicle in order to make sure that he had not run anyone over. Finally he stopped driving altogether. But it did not end there. Soon he could not leave his house, but then his immediate domestic surroundings became filled with terror; even opening a jam jar in the morning became a risk that something terrible would escape and do great harm to other people. During the course of his therapy these thoughts of catastrophe intensified until he felt that he could not speak because he believed that when he breathed words into the air something terrible was escaping from him that would harm others.

Over a period of eighteen months, in an intensive programme of day hospitalization, Andrew began to recover. The progress of therapy was faltering and difficult and involved an initial programme of medication cessation. The suspension of medication was testing to the extent that during the earlier phase of his therapy he became depressed with suicidal thoughts. The medication had perhaps masked these feelings. There did seem to be some elements of psychological dependence on the drug, and in many ways the ritual of taking the drug had become obsessive in its own way. In the main the combination of social and group psychotherapy meant an intense exposure to the interpersonal relationships in the treatment community. These experiences confronted Andrew with the very experience of intimacy that his OCD defended against. Inasmuch as his delusions had over time reduced all elements of social interaction to close to zero, therapy was a process of agonizing re-socialization. He did become extremely depressed and suicidal during his recovery as his obsessions abated, and some of his unconscious homicidal rage was transformed and identified in relation to conscious ordinary relationships with family, peers, and therapists. He was eventually able to return to work, though not in an occupation that involved driving.

In another case of OCD, that had a less successful outcome, Doris in her late 40s was obsessed about keeping everything clean and ordered at home. Her bed sheets had to be pristine, clothes ironed, everything had its place and was to be unmoved on shelves, and so forth. Her obsessive behaviour had become a source of great tension in her marriage and her family, and she was referred by her GP who felt she was depressed. Doris had great difficulty throwing anything away. The refuse bin was a source of much of her anxiety. She said she had a recurring vision that a sharp tin would cut the "bin man". It was very difficult to get her to think about where this lacerating thought might come from. She spoke of the thought as if it were not her own. During the course of her therapy it became apparent that this rather damaging vision masked other ideas that she harboured about doing damage to other people. She would close her eyes when talking about her feeling and imaginings, as if somehow this would "make them go away", so she said. In attempting to engage with her in therapy I experienced any attempt to stretch out to her as cut off before it reached her. I felt that I was cut like the bin man. It was hard to get Doris to look beyond her veneer, the image of herself as an amiable, lovable mother, wife, and friend. In one session, when asked what would happen if her husband moved his clean washing out of turn, she said she "would kill him". Although she said she "was being funny", I took this statement at face value. She became furious and stormed out of the session saying it was outrageous that she would want to kill her husband. Apparently on the way home she had walked into a gate and banged her head and had been concussed. I never saw her again and I received notice from her GP that she had decided that psychotherapy was not good for her.

It would appear that this dream world of delusion in OCD seems like a fixed state of mind that is comparable to the addicted mindset of the drug user, where the intoxicated world is perpetually in an altered dream state, and when not intoxicated existence is dominated by thoughts about the drug, how it is to be procured, and how it is to be ingested. The idea that one's thoughts are not one's own seems plausible; in a sense the mind is stolen by the drug, as Bion proposes. Bion's quote draws attention to the externality of the mind, the thought looking for a thinker. Doris's inclination was that her thoughts were external to her, that her rage somehow was not hers. Another patient with OCD illustrated the externality of thoughts most clearly in his presentation. Roger was often late for appointments because whenever he forgot what he was thinking about, he would need to return to the geographical location where he had had the thought in order to retrieve it. In other words, he felt that he had left his thoughts behind somewhere and would have to go back and pick them up. If he could not remember what he was thinking at a particular point in his journey he was overcome with such anxiety that something disastrous would happen, that he would keep repeating his foot-steps until he could remember what he was thinking. I saw him on a couple of occasions walking up and down roads nearby the psychotherapy department, as if fixed to the same small location. It was very painful to glimpse, even for a short time. Of course the ritual was not only deeply embarrassing, it meant that he was usually late for commitments. His life was severely debilitated by this compulsion.

Roger's ritual served to defend against intimacy. When he did manage to get to therapy he had a habit of disappearing into a fugue-like state. He would stay in this state until he was able to move his nose. When he became preoccupied with needing to do this his capacity to hear and speak was nil. Like Doris, he became cut off, almost non-conscious in relating to others.

With each of these cases I have a sense of the mind that is evacuated, that it becomes not of the self. The drug makes the mind numbed or estranged, and I concur with Bion that there is damage in the capacity to contain the dream, the dream exudes, and consciousness evaporates. And that this becomes a fixed state that takes over.

Dream fix

Consider the actual act of fixing in addiction. The fix is idealized, it is anticipated that it will "fix" a mental state that is felt to be wrong or broken. The addict gets his fix by putting the drug into his body, whether this is through smoking, swallowing, snorting, anal supposi-tories, or skin-popping. The injection, directly fixing into a vein seems to symbolize a desire for "umbilical attachment" (Rey, 1994). The needle attachment is equated as the giver of life and happiness. The addict wishes to be fixed permanently to his drug object. The drug is repeat-edly "ingressed" (sic) or engorged: a bodily process of absorption. Some injecting drug users will go to extreme lengths to get their fix: in the absence of a viable vein elsewhere, male addicts will inject into their penis, females into their breasts. Addicts will even inject into their eyes if necessary.

We might say that the primary drug object becomes an *encysted* body-mind object. Bion (1967, p. 47) uses the term "encyst" as a path-ological process and it seems apposite here inasmuch as it conveys a sense of toxic fusion where the ingress of the drug object may result in actual cysts, infections, septicaemia, endocarditis, and so forth. Simple primary objects become complex, doubly or multiply identified; as Rey (1994) has described, layer upon layer of confused objects converge in a network of psychotic relations. The drug becomes a fix of a psychotic object, confused and bizarre existing in an elaborate network of fantasy and conspiracy.

We might encounter the repetitive hallucination of the addict and OCD patient in the same way that a recurring dream is treated as a key window to the psyche in ordinary psychotherapy. One might add that the therapist needs to understand their own sleeping-wakefulness inasmuch as working with this repetitive material can be very soporific. When working with patients with OCD and substance abusers, I think it is fair to say that it can be soporific, as if Hypnos and Nyx are taking control. I have found myself on occasions feeling like I am rather talking in my sleep or perhaps sleeping in my talk. The danger of toxicity under the duress of such bludgeoning repetition ought to be accounted for in the preparation of practitioners. My thesis here is that the paradigm of health education and replacement prescribing has sleepwalked into the madness of repetition-compulsion. In a later chapter I describe the recurring attacks on the liver in the myth of Prometheus as an excellent metaphor for understanding the cycle of toxic object relations in drug addiction and I surmise that the therapist needs to be an active detoxifying agent, more like the liver than the alimentary canal, if they are to help patients discharge their toxic fixations (Winship, 1999). The capacity of wakefulness in the therapist should be a prerequisite towards self-preservation if the therapist is to avoid going mad too.

To summarize then, I would argue that the deployment of repeated hallucinatory points of *fixation* are clinically extant in psychosis, addiction, and OCD disorders. In each case there is a retreat from reality and a defence against intimacy. Obsessive-compulsive disordered patients get delusional *fixated thoughts* that impinge on social functioning where intimacy in relationship is averted to a preoccupation with things. Drug users get their *fix* where the mind-altered state can be characterized by recurring hallucinations and experiences which are re-capitulated only with increasing doses of their drug of choice. People suffering from psychosis have *fixed* delusions and hallucinations that remain remarkably consistent and unshifting. A unifying theory of psychotic repetition might be drawn from the complementary articulations as a basis of treating psychotic, obsessive-compulsive, and addictive disorders with a view to understanding and challenging social retreat, and finding new syntheses of sociality, initially in therapy and thereafter in recovery. This approach to psychotic fixation in addiction is a useful anchor for considering how treatment paradigms can be evolved which address the reflected madness of substitute prescribing.

CHAPTER TWO

Creation myths and breast junkies: in search of milk and honey

Opium of the masses

The private challenge of substance misuse is always a matter of political urgency even if it is not, as I discussed in the opening chapter, as Marcuse determined it. There is an alternative vista, arguably no less utopian than Marcuse's, but one that is more inclined to the mundane (clinical) than the profound (psychedelic). In distinction to the sociological positivism espoused by the likes of Durkheim (1952), who regarded progress as always solution focused, we might settle for something more reflective based on consciousness-raising with knowledge for knowledge's sake, austere rather than audacious. I want to suggest an object constant of study, a steady approach that piques curiosity, and sets out hypotheses about the nature of addiction.

My inquiry is circumscribed by the possibility that we might root out psychological theories about the urge to use drugs by returning to ancient myths where repetition-compulsion have been a feature. Myths are not straightforward of course, and the insight they offer is often coded. But when they are bundled together, read across time, and cross-checked with other independent myths, one can begin to discover congruent patterns. We see different myths telling the same stories. From

Mesopotamian to Celtic, from Aztec to Nordic, diverse cultures evolve analogous myths indicating commonality across cultures. Sometimes myths seem misleading and duplicitous. But it is possible to see strange stories and ancient transactions aggregating in collective meanings and morals, rules and rites of passage as J. G. Frazer (1922) demonstrated in his monumental work, *The Golden Bough*. The study of myths amounts to a sort of cultural archaeology where psychosocial phenomena can be interrogated to uncover constituents of the mind and human nature itself. Myths arise out of the sleepy daydream of a culture and become embroidered in the imagination of poets, writers, and storytellers. According to C. S. Lewis, myths tell something of great moment for all of us, some universal truth. For primitive man myths were the important means to explain what was fearful and unknown; gods and devils were created to explain the supply of food, the mysteries of death, and the idiosyncrasy of nature's elements.

The idea of using mythology to illustrate theories of the psyche was a staple technique for Freud (1913), who took his point of departure from J. G. Frazer. In Oedipus and later Narcissus among others, Freud detected the origins of a range of psychiatric presentations. From these ancient tales he developed an interpretative technique whereby the data from the stories could be shown to be representative of the clinical interior. Rather like dreams, Freud was keen to understand the universal basis of our mythical ancestry and how this might enlighten psychological theory.

In revisiting myths here, I likewise try to accrue knowledge about addiction, based on those aspects of the narratives which appear to unfold certain data about the human nature of intoxication and repetition-compulsion. The story of man's infatuation with intoxicants and the advancement of civilization is entangled with man's folly and preference for illusion over reality. It is an enduring problematic that did not escape Marx's attention when he saw the progress of equality for the masses floundering against the barricades of religious oppression. He likened the illusion of religion to the nullifying effect of opiates; religion was the opiate of the masses, he famously quipped. In the previous chapter I referred to Freud's (1930) aphorism about drugs as the "the drowner of cares", to his mind just as effective as religion in bringing about an illusory state of mind which sees people fleeing from the harsh reality of the world. Freud did not blame people for bowing down to the idea that there was some supernatural power that could be the source of redemption and nor was he overly critical of people who indulged in drugs. Freud understood that life was hard, and that our drive towards civility was always in the face of our urges in the other direction, our instinctive animal aggression, sibling rivalry, unruly sexual urges, and so forth. Drugs and religion were nonetheless "evils", said Freud, and they stood against civilization rather than progressed it.

There would seem to be a post-Freud-Marx atrophy between religion and drugs as a subject of investigation, that is to say there is very little investigation of religion and drugs as co-conspirators as suppressants of liberty. Actually it is not something that I feel able to debate too much here. Partly I do not feel that it is my business, rather it is more the case that those of a faith might illuminate the rest of us about their position. And partly my remit here is to concentrate on one particular half of the equation, that is drugs. But I would say that learning to live without religion might be like learning to live without drugs. I have worked with clients who have lost their faith, or renounced their religious beliefs altogether. In many cases the renouncement has been predicated by an existential crisis or significant loss of some description. The same might be said of people's trajectory when they give up drugs, that is to say, it is often prompted by some calamity or other. In the aftermath of drug and religious cessation there is a crisis of identity. For example, when people give up their repetitious acts of self-harm, they are led to ask, if I am not a drug user, then who am I? The same is said in the aftermath of giving up religion: if I am not a Muslim, a Christian, or a Jew, then who am I?

We are a world in crisis: economic, spiritual, the clash of civilizations, dwindling resources, population boom, and damage to the environment. A pandemic of drug misuse would seem part of, or a symptom, of global crisis. So what does this prompt? Will it prompt us to become sober? Unlikely! Imagine, a world without drugs, and no religion too (to borrow a line from John Lennon). It might seem unthinkable to envisage a godless world, a sort of stoical Utopia of ennui; a world without magical spirits, immortals, devils, or divinities. We need magic and myth to hold us together; stories can enthral us, teach children about the world in small doses. It would be erroneous to have a world without childhood majestic fantasies of creation, scientific, religious, or otherwise. But these dreams should be assigned to their rightful place as filial pedagogy. When these ideas remain compressed into maturity, then we are in trouble. It is an important step to understand that Santa Claus is not real. The advancement of genetics, the cloning of cells to create replica organisms, artificial insemination, and so on are medical advancements of note, but these achievements can become factitious to the point of a hyper-reality where all the ills of the world can be cradled in the arms of the biological laboratory creator-inventor who breaks the wondrous limits of our destiny. These too are the illusions created by drugs; we have entire systems of research hegemony funded by the dream that there is a medical solution to human emotional suffering.

Myths and stories can tell us about our folly. We should heed Mary Shelley's modern tale of Frankenstein as a motif for the aspirations of science and its ethical limits. Dr Victor Frankenstein recognized the horror of his perverse deed immediately, much as J. Robert Oppenheimer on hearing the devastating success of his atomic bomb quoted a fragment he remembered from the Bhagavad Gita: "I am become Death, the destroyer of worlds." The twentieth century might well be remembered as the pharmaceutical epoch, that emerged concurrently with the most violent century ever where the atrocious scale of scientific advancement saw a counterpoise of unprecedented destruction in genocide and war. The Greeks would tell the story of the goddess Artemis who was said to have the power to wipe out an entire city with one single arrow. When the atom bomb wiped out Hiroshima, it demonstrated that mortals had the power of gods after all; the myth of Artemis had become reality. We will probably develop even more power to inflict damage than even the gods our ancestors once imagined. When myths become prophecies ...

Far worse than Epictetus, Hobbes, Locke, Marx, Darwin, Nietzsche, and Freud, all of whom seem to be, to some extent at least, philosophers of pessimism, mankind's ever-competing interests and ideologies seem to risk tearing apart the fabric of the world with ever-greater momentum. Indeed, we live in a world ever-more capable of its own utter annihilation. Mass death and destruction has hovered so closely above the head of civilization lately, perhaps specifically since the Cuban missile crisis, that it must have by now impinged on the universal unconscious of post-Second World War generations. The extent of this imprint is yet to be fully comprehended. Horowitz (1957) asked the question as to what might be "the specific mechanisms, the forms evolved for coping with the threat of world conflagration" (p. 2). Perhaps we need look no further than the global drug epidemic.

It strikes me that there may be an axiom about the massive escalation in the conspirators of illusion that are either manifest in drug or religious fundamentalism. Drug use and religion are symptoms of a culture responding to trouble and trauma. Fundamentalism as a defining battleground between Muslims, Christians, Hindus, and Jews suggests that for many, god is far from dead, as Nietzsche foretold. It is land, oil, class, poverty, and prestige that are the real issues at stake, and will be for the foreseeable future. These can be submerged by the invocations of the competing claims that it is the will of some god or other that times have unfolded this way. In these dangerous and terrifying times our leaders turn to godheads to evoke comfort for the polity, but more importantly it is through their "spiritual calling" that they get leverage for political gain with oppositional pacifists who can than be charged with behaving inhumanely for not fighting the good fight. Maybe those who do not have god, choose drugs. Both seem to be dangerous illusions. For those who witnessed the British prime minister Blair's religious convictions influencing his political convictions in his decision to slay thousands of innocent Iraqi people ("I will be judged by my maker") is no less terrifying than the idea of holy Jihad. Bush's "God Bless America" rhetoric in opposition to Bin Laden's "Praise be to Allah" was deeply divisive to a world that would seem at times to be no more intellectually advanced than our ancestors who believed that it was gods who caused thunderstorms. Religion becomes a subtle but powerful weapon of terror. It may be that we are too close to the horrors of modernity to fully assess what we have become; it may only be in generations hence that historians can truly unpick the terrible wonders of creation and destruction in the twentieth century.

Creation myths

The film *Gridlock'd* (1997), directed by Vondie Curtis-Hall, follows the escapades of two New York heroin addicts and their attempt to join a methadone-maintenance programme. The film is an apocryphal tale that captures something essential about the discourse of drug rehabilitation in the later twentieth century. Stretch (played by Tim Roth) and Spoon (played by Tupac Shakur) are two musicians who decide that they went to get themselves into a rehab programme after a series of traumatic events that conspire to turn their lives upside down.

First their singer girlfriend nearly dies after an overdose, and then they are shot at while trying to score. Stretch has a gun held at his head for using the term "nigger" during an exchange with a black acquaintance and Spoon pleads with the man with the gun that Stretch is as "black as the next man".

After abortive attempts to get into a programme we see Stretch and Spoon at home slumped in their chairs watching a gospel television programme where the preacher, Skip Woods, is claiming: "Breast feeding in public is downright disgusting." He then adds: "Addicts, do we really want to give them clean needles?" At first it does not seem clear as to what is the point of compressing breastfeeding and addicts' clean needles. We might think that it could just be a coincidental juxtaposition. However, a short while later the point is pressed home when we see Stretch and Spoon walking across the concourse of a New York railway station. There is a slow motion sequence where Stretch looks over to a mother sitting on a bench breastfeeding her baby. This sequence is cut, albeit very briefly, with a close-up shot of a syringe with a moist needle tip. The conflation of the breast and the needle is therefore intentional, and not merely a coincidence of editing. We are alerted to a sort of breast-junkie proposition: is the director suggesting that there is a primary hunger for milk that explains the addictive urge in heroin misuse?

It might seem like a long shot, but in a nutshell however, this is the hypothesis that I want to explore herein. That the addictive appetite returns us to a milky paradise that has at once either been lost, or never really found. But before I look further into this I want to set an atavistic scene or two. It is known that mind-altering substances were burned in ancient rituals in Mesopotamia and Egypt, but naturally occurring herbaceous plants will have most certainly been ingested and burned long before. We might say that the rendering of ancient myths and tales of intoxication have been cast from a deep interlace between homo sapiens man and his use of mind-altering substances. Notably, it is in the comity of myths, folklore, and tales of birth and renewal, across continents and religions, where we see the concept of creation, including the creation of the universe itself, embedded on occasions in the narrative of mankind's experience of intoxication.

For instance, in the ancient Hindu myth it is said that while the god Shiva (also known as Siva) churned the Milky Way, creating the cosmos, the natural herbaceous hallucinogen hashish was born at the same time.

It is also told that while creating the cosmos, Shiva held the poison of the world in abeyance in his throat. Thus the birth of the universe in the Hindu myth holds a tension between the hashish ecstasy of drug ingestion on the one hand and the idea of holding at bay a poisonous destructive counterpoise. In many myths Shiva, lord of the cosmic dance, naked ascetic and symbolized most commonly in the form of a phallus, bears a resemblance to Dionysus. Both Shiva and Dionysus are known to be gods who bring much joy as well as destruction.

Like the Hindu myth, there is a Greek creation myth that also tells of the creation of the Milky Way. When Hera, wife of Zeus, was breast-feeding the infant Hercules, it was said that Hercules drew with such might upon Hera's breast that she was caused great pain which made her fling him off her breast. It is said that the milk from her breast then spurted out across the skies forming the cosmic spectacle of the Milky Way. As in the myth of Shiva, the ecstatic creation of the cosmos is combined with pain and destruction. Hercules grew up to be a beleaguered hero whose attempts at completing death-defying tasks were often confounded by his over-indulgence of alcohol, revivifying the intoxication of which he was deprived in infancy.

The story of the birth of Dionysus also has echoes of motherly abandonment. Semele, a mortal whom Zeus had bedded, gave premature birth to Dionysus and died in giving birth. Faced with the responsibility of caring for his motherless son, and fearing the jealousy of his wife Hera, Zeus hid Dionysus in his thigh. He later gave what was "second birth" to Dionysus. Dionysus's destiny was to become god of the vine, and like Hercules, was ordained to a life of intermittent drunkenness. That Zeus's son should be subject to intoxication seemed to replay a strand of family lineage, insofar as Zeus's triumph over his father Kronos occurred when Kronos was drunk on the honey of wild bees, at which point Zeus seized the chance to castrate his father. Zeus apprehended his place as king of the gods, marrying his mother Hera to seal the covenant. Given that Dionysus was motherless we might say that Zeus was spared the same fate as his father because with Semele's death any father-son competition for the desires of mother was eradicated. Thus Dionysus was not exposed to the jealous wrath of his father who may have otherwise felt usurped by Semele's love for her infant son. Instead, Zeus rather tenderly protected Dionysus who, being reborn was fed regularly by nymphs who, acting as surrogate primary carers, sprinkled his lips with honey. Later, the ground upon which Dionysus's maenads danced was said to have flowed with milk and honey, the food of his infancy. The mead of honey bees, like the vine, became the intoxicants of Dionysus that symbolized the loss of his mother but the acquisition of the surrogate food of the gods.

In the Bible there is the famous re-creation myth of Noah, who built a great ark to save the animals of the earth after God had decided to punish man by flooding the earth and killing everyone except Noah and his family who was selected to be the start of the new family of man. It is said that after the flood Noah planted a vineyard, and when there was a yield he made wine, but became drunk: "Noah, the tiller of the soil, was the first to plant a vineyard. He drank of the wine and became drunk, and he uncovered himself within the tent" (Genesis 9: 20–21). The sons of Noah, unlike the children of Kronos, did not castrate their father when they found him naked and drunk. In some ways Noah replays Adam's original act of "madness" in defying his god when he steals the cherished fruit from the tree of knowledge. The apple, grape, and honey have resonant religious symbolic connections (in the form of cider, wine, and mead) perpetuated in various rituals of Christianity.

The overflow of milk and honey is a feature in Samuel Taylor Coleridge's famous poem *Kubla Khan*, based on the mythical kingdom of Xanadu and the creation of a stately pleasure dome. It is well known that Coleridge wrote the poem after a vision when he had ingested several grains of opium. Coleridge gave fair rein to his drug appetite with his use of laudanum, a popular concoction during thenineteenth century that combined alcohol and opium. Laudanum was legal and in widespread use, particularly in the Suffolk Fens in the UK where opium plant cultivation was prolific. Thomas De Quincey (1907), another famous Victorian opium eater, was critical of Coleridge's denial of his acquaintance with opium. Others were keen to protect Coleridge's reputation, for example Joseph Cottle (1847), friend and literary contemporary asked:

> Is it expedient; is it lawful; to give publicity to Mr Coleridge's practice of inordinately taking opium? To soften the repugnance which might, pardonable, arise in the minds of some of Mr C's friends, it is asked, whether it be not enough to move abreast of adamant, to behold a man of Mr Coleridge's genius, spellbound by his narcotic draughts? (pp. 348–349).

In a letter to Thomas and Josiah Wedgwood in 1803, Coleridge had been candid about his appetite for mind-altering substances: "We will have a fair trial of Bang. Do bring down some of the Hyoscyamine pills, and I will give a fair trial of Opium, Henbane and Nepenthe. By the by I always considered Homer's account of the Nepenthe as a banging lie" (p. 464). Homer had written about nepenthe, which was probably hemp or opium blended with wine, and was used by Arabian physicians during operations. According to Homer, Polydamna, wife of Thonis who was king of Egypt, gave *nepenthe* to Helen, as "an antidote to grief and rage, inducing oblivion to all ills". It is not clear why Coleridge considered Homer's account a "banging lie", but one deduces that Coleridge's forceful opinion is gleaned from his own experience.

The reverie in which *Kubla Khan* was composed was supposedly induced after Coleridge had consumed several grains of opium in order to combat the worst effects of dysentery. Coleridge tells us that the fragment that remained of the whole vision was only a few hundred words. The drug reverie had seemingly evoked an image of a feeding euphoria, a stately pleasure dome overflowing with milk and honey, a vision of paradise so powerful that Coleridge had set about writing the poem almost immediately upon regaining consciousness. The poem took the story of Kublai Khan, born in 1214, grandson of the fierce warrior Genghis Khan, as its point of departure. Kublai failed in his attempt to extend the empire of the Mongol dynasty, but is known to have organized and ruled China with centralized taxes and improved agriculture. He built a beautiful palace complete with lush gardens in Cambaluc (now Beijing), which welcomed foreign traders including Marco Polo. He called the palace K'ai-p'ing, which translates into something sounding like "Xanadu".

In Coleridge's vision he journeyed across "fertile ground", "through crevices measureless to man", down to a "deep romantic chasm" where he found "woman wailing for her demon lover". If there were any doubts about the sexual motif in the poem, Coleridge pressed home the point with:

> As if this earth in fast thick pants were breathing,
> A mighty fountain momentarily was forced:
> Amid whose swift half-intermitted burst,
> Huge fragments vaulted like rebounding hail.

The imagery was a thinly veiled metaphor, almost adolescent in some ways, but perhaps rightly hailed as one of the greatest poems in the English language. From the cleavage of the milky breast to the vaginal ecstasy below and the frothy ejaculation, in the end the sated infant (an intoxicated Coleridge) lays sleepily swimming to the gentle strains of a dulcimer, "for he hath fed on the milk of paradise".

Such was the extent of Coleridge's use of opium it would be errone-ous to say that *Kubla Khan* was his only opium poem. Coleridge used opium continuously and with increasing regularity from the age of nineteen until his death at the age of fifty-two. It might be fair to say that there are probably few poems that were not composed or redrafted without some influence of an opium-altered state of mind (Lefebure, 1977). But *Kubla Khan* was exceptional in directness.

Coleridge's drug-induced vision of milk has echoes in Jean Cocteau's (1933) book *Opium*. Cocteau, French writer, artist, and film-maker, made numerous references to the relationship between milk and his hunger for opium when he described his experience of addiction and his attempts, mostly futile it seems, at withdrawal. In his journal *Opium*, we see several sketches that Cocteau drew during his periods of withdrawal. The fig-ures are all characterized by the fact that body parts have been replaced by smoking pipes. The hands, fingers, feet, and head have all become pipes which appear to be reaching out, resembling open-mouthed pores, vessels through which Cocteau's desire for opium might be greedily quenched. The sketches suggest that Cocteau was craving so much for his opium that people ceased to be people and became only pipes. Coc-teau likened his hungry drug craving to:

> Imagine a silence equivalent to the crying of thousands of children whose mothers do not return to give them the breast (1930, p. 57).

His attempts at temperance proved to be less than resolute and he knew he was at the mercy of his Morpheus muse: "It is useless my dear poet to assume this careless air. I shall smoke again if my work requires it" (p. 186). And his journal charts a familiar to and fro of rehab and relapse. However, he recorded his hope that one day there may be a medical solution and that:

> ... doctors will discover the hiding places of morphine and will draw it out by means of some substance for which it is greedy, as a bowl of milk attracts a serpent (1930, p. 9).

Like Coleridge, Cocteau summoned up a filial if not archaic image, that harked back to those earlier creation myths, of a milky appetite. Cocteau later proposed a quasi-scientific axiom arguing that:

> Milk, [is] the antidote to morphine. A friend of mine detests milk. When she was injected with morphine after an operation she asked for milk and liked it. The following day she could no longer take it (1930, pp. 22–23).

There is another piece of milk evidence in William Burroughs's *Naked Lunch* (1959), which like most of Burroughs's writings, is drawn from his life-long habit of using opiates. In the *Naked Lunch* Burroughs's corporeal alter ego and drug pimp Dr Benway is responsible for many despotic acts including teasing a man who is desperately craving for milk chocolate:

> Benway takes the chocolate bar from his pocket, removes the wrapper and holds it in front of the man's nose. The man sniffs. His jaw begins to work. He makes snatching motions with his hand, saliva drips from his mouth and hangs off his chin in long streamers. His stomach rumbles. His whole body writhes in peristalsis. Benway steps back and holds up the chocolate. The man drops to his knees, throws back his head and barks. Benway tosses the chocolate. The man snaps at it, misses, scrambles around on the floor making slobbering noises. He crawls under the bed, finds the chocolate and crams it into his mouth with both hands (1959, p. 39).

An array of creatures, some real like bugs, some composite, thread their way through *Naked Lunch*. Bug powder is the metaphor for opium. We are introduced to a "Mugwamp" creature whose function it is to supply an addicting fluid to clients otherwise known as reptiles. This fluid has the power to slow metabolism and therefore extend life and is secreted from erect protrusions on Mugwamps. Burroughs tells us that the Mugwamp is a creature without a liver who lives on only sweets. Reptiles suck translucent coloured syrups through alabaster straws: "A number of these [Mugwamps] flow over chairs with their flexible bones and black pink flesh. A fan of green cartilage covered with hollow erectile hairs through which the Reptiles absorb the fluid sprouts from behind each ear" (1959, p. 54). In the film version of *Naked Lunch* (1991), directed by David Cronenburg, the Mugwamp is shown to be a hybrid of a fat featureless alien pig-like creature with a long giraffe-like neck and the udders of a cow. The scene is set in a warehouse in Tangiers, resembling the opium dens that were ubiquitous there in the 1950s. We see numerous reptile-addicts crouching under the belly of the amoebic-like Mugwamps who are suspended limply above the ground like meat hanging from hooks in a slaughterhouse. The reptiles are greedily suckling on the teat-like protrusions of the Mugwamps, salivating and grappling with each other for a turn. A milky white fluid is the object of their desire.

The relationship between milk and intoxication was inculcated with a drink called Alcomilk that was marketed in the late 1990s. Alcomilk, to put it simply, seemed to appeal to the idea of getting drunk on milk. Although the same might be said of Bailey's Irish Cream (a mix of cream and whisky), Alcomilk and other drinks called "alcopops" were directed at an adolescent market and, as some believed, at an underage market. Alcomilk was withdrawn in 2003. In Spike Lee's (1995) film *Clockers* about crack dealing in Brooklyn, New York, the central character Strike was addicted to a drink called Moo, an alcomilk. Strike deals crack, but he does not use the drug himself, though it becomes apparent to us that he is addicted to Moo. When Strike does not have his Moo he suffers from stomach cramps and when he begins to produce copious amounts of blood in his sputum we surmise that he is suffering from a stomach ulcer. Addiction to crack is parodied with Strike's addiction to Moo.

Breast junkies

The archetypal imago of the addict, as someone who is gaunt and suffering from malnutrition, accurately portrays the physical condition that is rent from a range of addictions to mind-altering substances. One of the most common indicators of recovery and health improvement after addicts have ceased using, detoxified, and have begun to take steps towards sobriety, is that weight gain is a nigh-on ubiquitous clinical feature. This was the case, almost without exception, in the several hundred or so patients I observed undergoing drug detoxification and initial recovery. It is well known that putting on weight is often an unwelcome consequence for people giving up smoking, indeed smoking is sometimes a defence against weight gain. Many people speculate that the increased ingestion of food following the cessation of tobacco is about "something to do with your hands and mouth".

The return of appetite is sometimes credited to an increase in anxiety and agitation. It is as if there is a need to feel something inside; where once there was smoke there is a desire for the comfort offered by ingesting food, or where once there was heroin there needs to be milk, as Cocteau so eloquently put it.

One might perhaps argue that malnutrition in drug use is not so much a question of appetite but rather a socio-economic consequence of addiction insofar as food rates low on the scale of priorities; for many drug users money is prioritized for scoring drugs rather than buying food. However, the economics of using are not enough alone to explain the choice of drugs over food. Addicts who use prescribed drugs, and therefore do not have financial constraints, still suffer from under-nourishment. The widespread use of drugs in the fashion industry is well known. During the 1990s there was a trend known as "Heroin Chic" which was emblematic of the bearing of a group of models "fashionably" emaciated. The tag Heroin Chic referred of course to the use of appetite suppressing drugs. A physiological explanation of appetite suppression must be the first rationale for a shift in appetites from food to drugs.

Cannabis might be seen to be the exception here where the ingestion of cannabis has been well known to advance what is commonly known as "the munchies": an irresistible urge to devour food. Indeed, the action of cannabis as an appetite stimulant has been researched as to its therapeutic potential with both cancer and HIV sufferers where appetite stimulation has been clinically indicated. So far cannabis has been found to be clinically effective in preventing the nauseous side-effects of intensive chemotherapy treatment and some practitioners have been experimenting with prescribing cannabis for other disorders including anorexia. At first glance the phenomena of increased appetite would not appear to fit a hypothesis about drug use creating a sensation of being well fed and the experience of withdrawal evoking a need to be feed. However, my impression is that it is not so much the intoxication of cannabis that prompts an appetite, rather it is the state of withdrawal that evokes the urge to fill the space with food. After the initial effect of intoxication of cannabis the user begins to experience an altered mind state which is of lessening intensity. It is here that the desire for further ingestion follows.

The idea that addiction can be understood psychologically to be an "oral disorder" is not new, although my thesis here proposes a specific connection between breast, milk, and addiction. Clinically extant theories of addiction in relation to the type of primitive or infantile appetite have been available since the earliest psychoanalytic papers on addiction. The Hungarian analyst Sandor Rado (1926) referred to the experience of intoxication as the invocation of an "alimentary orgasm". Even in cases where drug ingestion was not oral, said Rado, as in the case of injectors, it was still possible to advance the idea that the pathology of addiction harked back to a fixation at an oral stage of development. A theory of an infantile feeding state evoked by drug use was Herbert Rosenfeld's (1965) assertion insofar as he proposed that intoxication for the addict was akin to the succour of the ideal breast in the mind of the user and an effort to rekindle the satisfaction of the earliest feeding experience.

Rosenfeld noted that the earliest attempts at re-creating the idealized feeding situation were apparent in the thumb-sucking activities of infancy and repetitious drug use became an adult form of thumb-sucking, that is to say an auto-erotic act that seeks the diminishment of bad feelings and rekindles an imagined connection with a feeding or comforting mother. Kohut (1977) concurred that the motivation behind intoxication was an attempt to reproduce the experience of being fed and sated. Furthermore Kohut (1977) observed that there was a likely link between a problem with maternal empathy during the first year of life and drug addiction later on in life. He suggested that drug use was a re-enactment of the desire for the lost or absent mother.

These corrugations of psychoanalytic theory are highly speculative and can only ever be advanced as hypotheses. However, there would appear to be at least some significant correlation in my foregoing debate with myth and popular culture where milk is the common thread. Taking the evidence and the theoretical speculation together, we are pointed in the direction that a primitive feeding state might lie at the heart of cases of severe and chronic addiction. Developmental or depth psychology has been the chosen explanatory level for myth interpretation in the modern era. I am in broad agreement with Campbell's (1959) notion that myths suggest ubiquitous imprints of experience. For example, Campbell argues that the universal fear of darkness in childhood arises from the trauma of transition from the womb to the light of birth. I am not sure that I would fully agree: surely the fear would be of the light, not the prior safety of the darkness, but I at least concur that there are universals of experience imprinted on us from the beginning of life. We might at least hypothesize that drug hunger is a manifestation of a deeper layer of hunger for a primary relational exchange, that is to say, there is a connection between craving for drugs and a craving for something that a mother can give a child. The myths mentioned at the outset of this chapter, of Dionysus and Hercules torn from their mother, are therefore exemplary that the desire for intoxication can at some psychic level be correlated with the loss of mother.

I suggest we consider that there is evidence of an elemental relationship between food and drug appetites. Physically and psychically users report that a drug-induced state evokes the feeling of being fed and sated. Drug intoxication often takes the individual beyond other biological desires, for instance to have sex or fulfil any other organic excretory need other than to succumb to the allure of the substance. On the other hand, withdrawal from a drug leads to an experience of hunger or desire for the substance which would ease the physical and psychic agitation that accompanies the withdrawal syndrome. It has often been noted that users who inject report that when they are withdrawing they chew on the rubber bung of their syringe. If the opening thesis in *Gridlock* is correct—that the breast and the needle are hungered in parallel—perhaps the chewing on the bung (technically called the "teat") evokes the imagined experience of the nipple in the mouth. The chewing of the bung is on the one hand a reassuring act for the addict as he waits for the next ingestion of his chemical breast food, and also perhaps an agitated or frustrated biting because the elixir of satiability is not forthcoming.

Civilization and its discontents

So how might a formulation about drug hunger relate to the prologue in this chapter about the context of drug use in civilization? Dionysus is the mythical god of choice that we might here invoke to guide us. He provides us with a model of "arrival", the birth of the new season where fruits grow and honeybees collect nectar. The Dionysian cycle of new arrival brings with it another facet of the Dionysus myth, that of indestructibility. The sated Dionysian god-child feels that life will last forever. Such is the state of mind of the addict who feels immortal, powerful, and indestructible. It is of course utter madness to contemplate immortal life even for the briefest moment. Dionysus is thus the "mad-god" as Homer calls him, not just mad himself but also for the effect he has on others. In considering these interchanging components in the mythical cycle of the intoxicating Dionysus we can begin to root out the nature of addiction to mind-altering substances as the ever renewing desire for creation counterpoised by the recurring threat of death. It is towards a theory of death instinct in addiction that we need to develop our understanding; this is where we begin to unfold the psychological intricacies of drug ingestion at the point where euphoria touches destruction and death. This is the impetus for the following chapters.

CHAPTER THREE

"Dracula": from Stoker's classic of compulsion to Arthur's dark room

Brief

The myth of vampirism, especially retold in Bram Stoker's (1897) classic gothic tale *Dracula*, offers us a compelling account of obsession. With insights beyond many text-books, Stoker's *Dracula* is arguably indicative reading for any student studying addiction and compulsive disorders. The tale of *Dracula* weaves together many common threads of repetition-compulsion, and is of especial relevance in terms of the elements of allure, danger, and death. It is not uncommon for addicts to tell stories of their binges, recounting their close calls with death with some relish. The imago of the sickly pale addict whose relentless drug habit is draining him of his life and drawing him ever downwards towards death has become something of a cultural icon for the tragedy of modernity. The perpetuity of Prometheus's punishment, bound to a rock, having his liver devoured every day by a vulture, like the tale of *Dracula* suggests to us the cycle of living death, and this is the central theme I explore over the next chapters. But I begin here with Arthur, my client who asked a question that set the frame for this chapter.

Arthur's theorem

It had been over communal dinner on the inpatient unit, 1988, when Arthur, a young cocaine user asked me: "Gaz, why is it that so many addicts are into Dracula?" At the time I was stumped. For a start I did not know that so many addicts were, and I was not sure whether this was a subject to chew on at dinner anyway. But it was a question that came to keep my attention subsequently, as well as having some relevance to Arthur's therapy. Arthur was twenty-one and several weeks through his recovery programme. He was beginning to be curious about himself in a way that gave reason to be hopeful that he was readying himself for a shot at abstinence. He was gaunt, bright, and resourceful and I liked him a good deal. His heavy glasses would balance precariously on his nose and the lenses would make his eyes looks extraordinarily large, accentuating a searching and sometimes penetrating gaze. His talk was darting and often hard to follow, even when he was sober. But when I had first assessed him as an intoxicated outpatient he had spoken at such speed that he was almost incomprehensible. He had spent endless days and nights watching films like *Eraserhead* and *Blue Velvet* with their motifs of dark sexual repression. *Dracula*, as I discovered, also had a sharp erotic undertow that must have appealed to his cultural taste buds.

Arthur had been brought up in an era when poorer inner cities in the UK were in decline, the collapse that lent impetus to the idea later of inner city regeneration. Under the Tory administration during the 1980s comprehensive education had not so much been neglected as rather assaulted. It was a harsh world to grow up in, with a struggling state education system and rising unemployment. Arthur's descent into addiction was all too familiar. By then drug addiction had begun to show signs of the epidemic proportions subsequently realized in the 1990s. With unemployment running at more than three million during the five years since Arthur had left school, his drug habit was a sort of political rejoinder to the depressing contemplation of a generation that seemed to feel it had "no future". The hatred of reality for Arthur, and many of his friends, was eased by the regularity of chemical escapism. But when the drugs stopped working, and perhaps even making things worse, Arthur began looking for a way out. He wanted to be a journalist, a writer, or photographer, something in the media. I could not see why not—if he could re-channel the energies he had spent propping up his addiction over the previous four years. I respected his street-wisdom, he understood well his predicament and those of others around him, and though he was too wired to allow me to spend much more than fifty minutes a day listening to him, I nonetheless learned a great deal from him.

Arthur managed his detoxification and began to engage in the process of exploratory therapy. He was determined to reinvent himself. His enthusiasm applied itself to learning about photography. He borrowed books from the library and was given a camera by a relative. He learned to develop his own photographs and after some reorganization of space on the ward Arthur was able to use one of the spare rooms as a darkroom where he started experimenting with images. There was something about his photographic negatives as they emerged from the darkroom that started to throw shards of light on the question of Dracula. I will say more about Arthur later, but first let me set the scene that is the backdrop to Arthur's supper time question: "Why is it that so many addicts are into Dracula?". But before we get to the count, let us first begin by meeting his mythical forebear.

Dionysus to Dracula

The Greeks appear to have been the first to incorporate intoxicants as festival rites and as a result no other god of antiquity compared to Dionysus could be said to have a more central role in the rituals of celebration. For the peasants who were involved in working in the agricultural regions of Greece, where material happiness depended on a good crop of vines, Dionysus and his circle of immortals represented a mini Olympus and a religion in its own right (Pater, 1895). In the religions of Dionysus we find refined narratives of tree-worship and celebration of the yield of plants, and in Euripides's *Bacchae* Dionysus comes to have a scope equal to that of the goddess Demeter; he is to the vine what she is to the grain and the abundance of riches of the earth are theirs to be gifted.

Although Dionysus is best known as the god of alcohol and intoxication, he is also closely associated with comic tragedy (Kerenyi, 1977). He is perhaps the most contradictory of all the gods. From the spirit that can be seen loosening the tongues of fine eloquence at grand banquets, to a flesh-devouring hunter, Dionysus is the embodiment of the labile dimensions of human nature. It is the anguish of his mortal mother

Semele, who dies during his birth, which installs the psychological substrate of the Dionysian tragedy. Myths of Dionysus traverse from the countryside and its agrarian origins into the town. In rural environs Dionysus is enthusiastic and uninhibited, meanwhile the urban Dionysus is more melancholic and sinister. The loss of the peaceful idyll of the countryside might be a metaphor for the loss of mother. The shift from rural to urban in the Dionysian cycle suggests a transition from outside to inside where the radiance of mother summer transforms into the darkness and chill of winter where one takes refuge inside. In winter, without the abundance of yield, the death of all sweet things and the threat of the cold, Dionysus is transformed into a beast seen storming wildly in the darkness:

> "This transformation, this image of the beautiful soft creature becoming an enemy of human kind … in his madness wronged by his own fierce hunger and thirst, and haunting, with terrible sounds, the high Thracian farms, is the most tragic note of the whole picture and links him on to one of the gloomiest creations of later romance, the were-wolf, a belief that still lingers in Greece …" (Pater, 1895, p. 47).

In these darker times, the sacred women of Dionysus eat flesh and drink blood and sacrifice a fair boy who is deliberately torn to pieces commemorating the lean pickings of the winter. The three daughters on Minyas devote themselves to Dionysus's worship, casting lots as to which one of them will offer up their own infant. They are then turned into bats, moths, and other creatures of the night. It is this motif of Dionysus that has resonances with the mythological characteristics of vampirism. Stoker's portrayal of Dracula's three maidens preying on a baby in lean times derives directly from the myth of Dionysus.

In the rebirth of the year, with the arrival of spring and the lightness of warmer days, Dionysus is seen recovering from the malady of his winter madness: the source of the celebratory *Bacchanals* of Euripides. Spring festivals of Dionysus turn from the darkness to the exuberance of new life, intoxication is rejoined with rituals of renewal with dance and music aplenty. While Apollo is the god of higher airs of stringed instruments, Dionysus rules over the earthier music of the reed, pipe, and woodwind. It is from Pan, one of his Satyrs, that the Shepherds of Theocritus receive the flute pipes. The music accompanying these celebrations is not the refined persuasions of other gods, but rather inclined towards wild choral singing, chanted or sung with rhythm referred to as "dithyrambic". It is said Dionysus's followers, the *dithyrambus*, sung celebrations of the double birth of Dionysus, the one glorious to the father, the other to the anguish of the death of his mother. The merging of music, comedy, celebration, and tragedy has remained an unshifting constant of Western civil culture and the role of alcohol in mediating human relations.

The riddle of Dracula

Dracula with his changeable moods in light and darkness, his aristocratic cordiality in surreptitious tow with his bestial appetite for blood, are all traits which resemble the immortal Dionysus. The mad and wild winter Dionysus would seem to be the prototype for the popular construction of the modern vampire. Published in 1897, Stoker's *Dracula* has become synonymous with the myth of vampirism.

There is, it should be said, ample evidence that Bram Stoker's circle of friends in the literary, theatrical, and artistic worlds were well acquainted with the habits of morphinism and the use of laudanum, the aqueous combination of alcohol and morphine which was taken widely in the latter half of the 1800s. Lizzie Siddal, the best favoured model and muse for Gabrielle Dante Rossetti of the pre-Raphaelite brotherhood and a neighbour of Stoker, died of an overdose of laudanum, and as we shall see, her death weaves it way into Stoker's story.

While we know Stoker was surrounded by morphinism there is no actual evidence, however, that he himself partook other than in the last few years of his life when he took morphine to nullify the pain of syphilis (Farson, 1975; Leatherdale, 1985, 1987; Ludlam, 1962). There would appear not to be a simple answer to Arthur's question about Dracula chiming for addicts because Stoker does not appear to be writing as the insider. However, in the novel there is more than a passing interest in the detail of drug use when Dr Seward records his use of "Modern Morpheus, C2 HC/30. H201". Seward records that he "must be careful not to let it grow into a habit" (p. 101). And there is some resemblance to the process of addiction in the characteristic sombre decline of the new vampire who becomes increasingly reliant on a fix of blood, much in the same way that the addict desires the fix of the needle, the drawing of the blood back from the vein and then the ecstasy of exchange of drug fluid with body fluid. *Dracula* in this sense suggests more than an acquaintance with addiction.

The "meaning" of Stoker's novel has been the subject of much debate. Stoker proves to be as illusive as the count himself. As Clive Leatherdale (1985) has suggested, there may be a hint that Stoker covered his tracks, destroying various personal papers before his death. The two fullest biographies of Stoker are by his grandson Harry Ludlam (1962) and by Daniel Farson (1975). Both compile the known facts about Stoker's life, his whereabouts at certain times, his friendships, and so forth, but neither seem to get much beyond the surface of the man. While each of the biographies observes the seedier side of the world that surrounded Stoker, neither identifies any vices with Stoker. He seems to have been an upright citizen, a quiet and restrained man pursuing a steady career as a journalist with some adroit. Stoker's main passion, if we can call it that, was saved for the theatre and his job of managing the famous actor Henry Irving, whose statue stands in the heart of London's theatreland just north of the National Portrait Gallery on Charing Cross Road. Stoker was best known in his day for his relationship with Irving and the fact that Stoker was the author of *Dracula* was of secondary import. It is the ups and downs of the theatre world and his relationship with Irving and the actor's famous circle of acquaintances that form the most substantial narrative in Stoker's biography.

Dracula is immersed in the macabre of human nature, and yet is incongruous with the impression we have of Stoker himself. We might wonder how someone seemingly straight-laced like Stoker produced such a brutal, erotic, and gruesome tale. If we accept that Stoker did in fact religiously abstain from engaging in any personal vices, we might take the novel itself as indicative of the repression of desire and what emanates from the strain of self-restraint. This indeed may be something of an epitaph of Victorian culture. *Dracula* has a good case to be an epoch defining novel, the epitome of the genre of the Victorian gothic novel. The same might be said for Robert Louis Stevenson's (1886) *Strange Case of Dr Jekyll and Mr Hide*. Stevenson's tale of a respectable Victorian medical apothecary who experiments with a new concoction discovering that ingestion leads to the release of a powerful dark side, Mr Hyde, is even more apparently a documentary about the perils of drug ingestion. Indeed, while writing the novel Stevenson had himself been experimenting with a new concoction called cocaine. He had used cocaine alongside his more regular use of opium and had discovered the new mind-altering effects of the mixture. He is said to have completed the writing of his novel, 65,000 words, in just six days.

Like *Dracula* the *Strange Case of Dr Jekyll* ... explores the interior and exploits especially the fear of losing control to one's animalistic intentions. The novel has a Darwinian overture in this sense, that is to say, man is descended from animal rather than reared in the idyllic Garden of Eden. We see how the dangerous Mr Hyde comes increasingly to overtake the moral servitude of Dr Jekyll until Hyde threatens to gain the upper hand in perpetuity. Apart from offering a possible allegory of the repressed undertow of upright Victorian social conformity, Stevenson also released a contemporaneous insightful vignette of "dementia praecox", a term coined by the psychiatrist Emile Kraepelin (1856–1926) describing organic psychic collapse resulting in madness. Dementia praecox was shortly to be incorporated in the taxonomy of psychiatry before being replaced later by the term "schizophrenia", literally meaning "split mind". The theory of schizophrenia, based on psychological and neurological advances in understanding, moved away from an endogenous model of organic pathology as an error of metabolism. Schizophrenia became the diagnostic category of choice to explain a manner of psychotic presentation among certain patients and Stevenson's split personality of Jekyll and Hyde provided a rich illustration of the clinical theorem.

But for all the merits of Stevenson's *Strange Case of Dr Jekyll and Mr Hyde*, Stoker's *Dracula* seems to have stood up better to the test of time. The enduring popularity of the aristocratic vampire myth suggests that it is not just to one generation that the tale speaks, but rather its appeal has carried across generations. *Halliwell's Film Guide* records more than 300 films about Dracula and the vampire motif, a number that far exceeds the number of films dedicated to any other single character, living or dead, fact or fiction. Vampires and Count Dracula lay firm claim to being *the* most cinematic characterization of our age, and that is before we start to assess the motif of vampires in television series from *Buffy the Vampire Slayer* to cartoons like *Mona the Vampire*. Andy Warhol described Dracula as one of the "great modern myths" (the other being "Superman", he said). Elisabeth Kostova's (2005) novel *The Historian*, based on a retelling of Stoker's *Dracula*, broke all records for a book advance and the film rights of the book were sold for a record figure.

The enduring reclamation of a myth as it is reproduced in stories, films, plays, novels, or other cultural artefacts, is some measure of how well it portrays issues of common importance. The longer a myth survives the greater relevance it can be said to have. Dracula is the case exemplar of this *par excellence*. In spite of many social and cultural drifts, the story of Dracula has remained compelling and can be now viewed as a collective motif of culture. Even if Stoker's novel is not explicitly conveying a tale about drug addiction, it nonetheless can stand as an inscription for the universal psychology of compulsion that has come to prominence in modernity. The drug epidemic of the late twentieth century and early twenty-first century can therefore be reviewed in light of this culture of compulsion as an abiding feature of modern life in all parts of the developing world. There are grounds to consider the interlace of the myth of vampirism and addiction not only as Arthur suggested in relation to the fascination of the drug addict, but also against the wider canvas of social reverie.

Stoker did not invent vampirism; myths about vampires and blood-letting existed in many cultures long before Stoker breathed new life into the idea. In *Dracula* Stoker brought together previous widespread anxieties about vampires and gave the legend a new lease of life. His approach to Dracula was not haphazard; rather it was a scholarly effort at creating a novel amalgam of mythology, legend, and folklore. Documentation unearthed in the 1970s at the Rosenbach Foundation in Philadelphia by Leatherdale (1987) show to us that Stoker had fastidiously researched his version of the tale. It was in the summer of 1890, on a visit to the local library while holidaying in Whitby, that Stoker first read about "Dracul" (sic), a Hungarian prince with a penchant for violently ruling his subjects. The book was by William Wilkinson (1820), *An Account of the Principalities of Wallachia and Moldavia*, and in it Stoker would have noted that the name Dracul when translated from Hungarian meant "devil". Thus the devil incarnate in Count Dracula was born in Whitby Library, a few miles south of Scarborough on the North-East coast of England.

Whitby is also the place in the novel where the count lands after he has ventured from his homeland. In setting the majority of the novel in England, with Dracula as the dangerous outsider, Stoker invoked a sort of xenophobic undertow. There may have been some amity here in the context of a guilty British Empire mentality, that is to say, it was the British who were guilty of invading other lands and not the reverse as Stoker devised. The threat of Dracula as the archetypal dark foreign invader is eventually countered by another archetypal outsider from Northern Europe, Professor Van Helsing, a Teutonic hero who in the end saves the day. Socio-cultural readings of the novel have emphasized its racial dimensions, noting the anti-Semitic characterization of the Jews described in Jonathon Harker's travels in the story. Other political interpretations have suggested that Dracula was a manifesto for Marxist economic theory, an allegory about the rich aristocracy sucking the lifeblood out of the poor. Indeed, in *Das Kapital* Marx had said that: "Capital is dead labour that, vampire-like, only lives by sucking … the blood of living labour" (chapter X). Other interpreters of the novel note that Stoker pays homage to a banal Christian triumph, the god-fearing men who conquer the devil incarnate.

The span of orthodox interpretations of the novel suggests that Dracula can be seen as a condensation of a whole range of intersecting concerns. The narrative sequence provides us with an interplay of socio-cultural events, beginning with Harker's own diary account at the beginning of the novel when he records his observations of the superstitious behaviour of the locals as he travels deep into the mountains to visit the castle of Dracula which he has been instructed to sell. And later there are recorded observations of Dr Seward of Renfeld who is incarcerated like a laboratory rat in the asylum. Stoker thus posits the observation of superstition and madness as a key device in the novel, that is to say, the reader is invited to become a co-investigator. Stoker appeals to our voyeurism, and like his contemporary Freud, he takes us to the depths of the human psyche. No matter how murky, Stoker signals that the novel will engage us in experimental psychology. As Seward records his observations of Renfeld:

> The attendant tells me that his screams whilst in paroxysm were really appalling. I can quite understand the effect, for the sounds even disturbed me though I was some distance away. It is now after dinner-hour of the asylum, and as yet my patient sits in a corner brooding, with a dull, sullen, woebegone look in his face. I cannot quite understand it. Later.—Another change in my patient. At five-o'clock I looked in on him and found him seemingly happy …. He was catching flies and eating them. He has the sugar of his tea spread out on the windowsill, and is reaping quite a harvest (p. 115).

We are wise to the fact, though Seward is not, that Renfeld's malady anticipates Count Dracula's arrival. This is a well-known transaction in successful horror films, where the audience are able to anticipate what is happening long before the characters in the film. Hitchcock deployed this with regularity in his movies. Stoker's caricature of the treatment of Renfeld does not seem to be accidental parody. The reader knows what is going on before the hapless Seward, but the reader is helpless to intervene. Stoker's interest in psychology here comes hot on the heels of Freud & Breuer's (1895) paradigm-shaking *Studies on Hysteria* which signalled the birth of psychoanalysis with in-depth case accounts. Both Stoker and Freud, in their own ways, were attuned to researching sexual perversions, both inclined to chart the descent of man into the darker depths of the primitive psyche, and both explicitly influenced by the physician Mesmer. Freud used hypnosis in his early experiments with his patients and Stoker endowed Count Dracula with similar skills of mesmerism over his victims.

But it is Freud's and Stoker's shared interest in sexual motifs that seems to stand out. Harker's encounter with the female vampires in the early part of the novel leave little to the imagination:

> The fair girl went on her knees and bent over me fairly gloatingly. There was a deliberate voluptuousness which was both thrilling and repulsive, and as she arched her neck she actually licked her lips like an animal, till I could see in the moonlight the moisture shining on the scarlet lips and on the red tongue as it lapped the white sharp teeth. Lower and lower went her head as the lips went below the range of my mouth and chin and seemed about to fasten on my throat. Then she paused, and I could hear the churning sound of her tongue as it licked her teeth and lips, and I could feel the hot breath on my neck. Then the skin of my throat began to tingle as one's flesh does when the hand that is about to tickle it approaches nearer—nearer. I could feel the soft, shivering touch of the supersensitive skin of my throat, and the hard dents of two sharp teeth, just touching and pausing there. I closed my eyes in a languorous ecstasy and waited—waited with beating heart (p. 38).

Ernest Jones saw *Dracula* in terms of a coded tale about the repressed procreative sexual act, although it is fair to say that these themes are barely coded. *Dracula* is crammed full with sexual titillation, fellatio, rape, necrophilia. Jones thought the blood might be symbolic of the menstrual cycle in women, Dracula's night flights the male equivalent symbolic of nocturnal emissions. Dracula's various later seductions are imbued with sexual intensity and the scene where Harker, Seward, and Van Helsing drive a stake into a female vampire resembles a sort of gang orgy with an unwilling victim. It is surprising given the climate of Stoker's day that the novel escaped Victorian censorship. Perhaps Stoker was beguiling in presenting perversions in a way that were discreet and camouflaged. It is also possible that people could not quite believe what they were reading. I imagine critics daring not to risk speaking out about the depravity for fear of drawing attention to themselves for thinking such things.

Most interpretations of *Dracula* focus on the heterosexual content of the narrative, that is to say, Count Dracula as the patriarch who sires his offspring with a blood bondage that becomes a mark of family. The battle of the brotherhood of Van Helsing, Harker, and Seward who chase Dracula and eventually destroy him in order to protect the womenfolk is emblematic of a traditional recounting of an Oedipal struggle: the sons who seek to triumph over the father in order to dispossess him of his hold over mother. However, more lately some of the undercurrents of latent homosexuality apparent in the novel have come to the fore: for example, the threat of Count Dracula's first ravishment of the young Jonathon Harker when he is held hostage at the castle, and also Dr Seward's trepanation (surgical boring and perforation) of Renfeld. The film version of *Dracula* (1998) starring Tom Cruise laid much greater emphasis on the homosexual undertow and was critically acclaimed by many as an accurate rendering of Stoker's latent intentions. Even putting aside the homosexual agenda, the male bravado throughout the novel reflected Bram Stoker's known intimacy and preference for the company of men in his life and his enduring relationship with Henry Irvine which spanned more than thirty years. It is generally considered that Stoker cast himself in the novel as the intrepid and faithful Jonathon Harker and that Henry Irving was the template for the count. The homoerotic undertow of Stoker's and Irving's relationship remains a reasonable source of supposition. Some reference has been made to the features of sexual repression apparent in Stoker's life. Stoker married Oscar Wilde's ex-wife and Leatherdale (1987) notes that from the time of the birth of their first and only child, Stoker's wife Florence supposedly became frigid. It is, however, plausible that it was Stoker who turned away from Florence and not the other way around. Given that history so often repeats itself it is possible that Florence may have found herself married to not one but two homosexually latent men.

We might say that the novel then emerges against the backdrop of not only Victorian sexual repression but also Stoker's own personal sexual conflicts.

Sex, death, and love bites: lingering at the door of Jocasta's chamber

Stoker's portrayal of necrophilia in the novel is, of course, key. There is a biographical anecdote which begins to inform us of Stoker's development of the theme, that is to say, the dangerous allure of the beautiful walking dead, and how this is linked to drug misuse. The biographical anecdote is this. One of Stoker's London neighbours was the Pre-Raphaelite artist Gabriel Dante Rossetti. Rossetti's wife Lizzie Siddal died in 1862 after an overdose of laudanum, the popular concoction of alcohol and opium. Lizzie was buried in Highgate cemetery along with a volume of her husband's poems. Presumably, either Rossetti thought that his poems would be of comfort to Lizzie as she set her course towards the afterlife, or he was intent on making a magnanimous public statement of his love for his wife. Several years later, however, Rossetti decided to have Lizzie's body exhumed, ostensibly in order that he could retrieve the poems! It was said that when the lid of the coffin was lifted, the corpse was perfectly preserved with Siddal's red hair apparently filling the grave. But when her body came into contact with the air, it began to decompose.

Stoker was apparently so impressed with this story that he used it as the basis for some of the cemetery scenes in the novel. The cause of Lizzie's death, a drug overdose, may have been coincidental to Stoker's ploy. On closer inspection, the nightmarish imagery in the novel does begin to show uncanny features of resemblance to the dreamy world of narcotic addiction. Anyone who has observed someone steadily plummet into opiate addiction may recognize certain features in Stoker's account of the descent into vampirism. This is particularly personified in the demise of Lucy, Dracula's first English victim. Unbeknown to her protectors Lucy becomes increasingly reliant on Count Dracula's visits:

> She eats well and sleeps well, and enjoys the fresh air; but all the time the roses in her cheeks are fading, and she gets weaker and more languid day by day; at night I heard her gasping as if for air.

She is paler than is her wont, and there is a drawn, haggard look
under her eyes which I do not like (pp. 94–95).

Lucy succumbs to an unquenchable desire for Count Dracula. The
aetiology of the obsessive need for blood increases over time until she
feels she cannot live without it. Here tolerance levels increase as more
and more of Dracula's blood is required to bring about homeostasis;
in a sense Lucy develops an unquenchable appetite for Dracula's blood
as she herself becomes a vampire addict. The precision with which the
count hits the vein on the neck is comparable to the surgical precision
of the hypodermic needle, although it is the count who is the source of
the addictive urge. When he begins his seduction of Mina we see the
reversal of appetite: it is not Dracula who desires blood but rather his
victims who require his blood. In the novel Dracula opens his shirt to
Mina and tears the flesh on his chest and then …:

> … his right hand gripped the back of the neck, forcing her down on
> his bosom. Her white night dress was smeared with blood, and a
> thin stream trickled down the man's bare breast. The attitude of the
> two had a terrible resemblance to a child forcing a kitten's nose into
> a saucer of milk (p. 282).

As in the earlier chapter where I proposed an explanatory model
describing addiction in terms of milk, and a disturbed primary feeding
euphoria, Stoker compels us to consider the filial relationship between
the teeth, the sucking urge, and the breast.

Let us consider then the possible theoretical yield of the psychodynamics of sucking and biting. Of course the blood is a key symbol
here. Indeed, Dracula appears to offer a slant on a traditional Christian
theme where the drinking of red wine is intrinsic to various ceremonies
evoking the last supper where the disciples exhorted Christ by symbolically drinking his blood. While Christians believe that through the
spillage of Christ's blood everlasting life is promised to all, Dracula's
blood symbolizes everlasting death and a reverse sort of immortality.
In this way Dracula is positioned as an Antichrist. But it is the biting
dynamic that brings with it fascination and fear. Dracula can often been
seen leering over his female victims as he bends down to sink his teeth
into the neck. The film versions of *Dracula* appears to invert the idea
that it is the male breast, Count Dracula's, that is the object of desire.

The cinematic template is the 1921 German film *Nosferatu*, the first film based on Stoker's novel. *Nosferatu* has a scene where the shadow of the talon hand of the vampire passes over the body of a sleeping female victim. As he closes in for the attack, the shadow of the sharp talons of his hand come to a halt as they hover over the breast before clasping shut in a final dramatic moment.

The best psychological theory of teeth and their role in tearing, biting, and sadistically attacking the breast comes from the work of Melanie Klein. It is a depth-psychology that offers a speculative schema for the infant's early encounter with mother. Klein is not for the feint-hearted and her searching work, it might be said, has much resonance with the timbre of Stoker's novel, often evoking a reaction of shock and horror in the reader. Klein's own analyst and teacher was Karl Abraham, one of Freud's most faithful lieutenants whose full promise and contribution to psychoanalysis was rather cut short with his early death at the age of fifty. Klein was deeply influenced by him and it could be said that Abraham was a Kleinian even before Klein knew she was. She continued to reference Abraham's ideas even in her final papers, some of which she dedicated to him. Abraham has been a rather underregarded figure in the history of psychoanalysis, but some of his papers are among the most fascinating in the field, progressing knowledge with novel insights going beyond Freud.

Abraham's (1913) paper, "Restrictions and Transformations of Scoptophilia in Psycho-Neurotics", is of particular interest because he described the treatment of a patient who was a creature of the night who could not bear sunlight. It might sound familiar to us! Abraham's photophobic patient protected himself from the sun by hanging heavy curtains. During the course of talking about this phobia the patient revealed to Abraham that he associated the sun with his father's watchful eye. This revelation in itself was unremarkable and led Abraham to formulate a familiar father-son Oedipal tension. But during subsequent discussions the patient told Abraham that from his adolescence onwards he had refused to acknowledge that his mother was beautiful. It was a prohibition he said he had consciously imposed on himself. The aversion to looking at his mother had become replayed in the patient's avoidance of looking at other women. This behaviour, which had become habitual, amounted to a significant root problem in his life, especially since he longed for and desired a relationship with a woman. It was fairly rudimentary therefore that he would need to get over his anxiety and start looking at women, Abraham determined. Abraham said to the patient that he thought that the sun represented not only father but also the resplendent beauty of his mother. He thought that the photophobia was a symptom of his childhood fear that if he looked at his mother his father would be angry and jealous. Hereupon Abraham reworked Freud's theory of castration anxiety, that the little boy was afraid of loving his mother for fear of retribution from the father. But Abraham's emphasis on the role of mother in this drama rather subtly shifted the emphasis away from father to mother.

Freud had always kept the father at the very centre of his investigations. But now, while paying due deference to the Oedipus complex citing Freud's understanding of scoptophilia (fear of looking at mother) as a blinding self-punishment, Abraham seemed to be asking what was it that Oedipus had seen in his mother? Whereas Freud had encountered Oedipus on the road overthrowing his father Laius, Abraham had followed Oedipus into Thebes where he observed Oedipus lingering at the door of his mother's chamber. Abraham referred to mother's rudimentary beauty; after all Oedipus must have had reason to fall in love and marry his mother.

In his next papers Abraham began to develop his ideas about the infant's relationship with mother. In the "The first pre-genital stage of the Libido" (1916), Abraham began by noting Freud's (1905) notion that early libidinal drive was not directed outwards at an external object but rather towards the self. Freud referred to this inward desire as "auto-eroticism", arguing that one of the first states of pleasure was derived from sucking where the mouth featured as an erotogenic zone. Abraham supported these findings but said that the oral stage of libidinal development needed further deconstruction. He introduced case material from the analysis of a patient suffering from schizophrenia, who seemed to have something of an addiction to milk. The patient described sucking his tongue and reported to Abraham: "It is like sucking at the breast" (1916, p. 255). The patient also told Abraham that when he craved milk he found that masturbation could ease the craving. Furthermore, the patient recounted a memory of a wish to bite into his wet nurse. Associations about meat and flesh led Abraham to advance a hypothesis regarding a "phantasy of biting into the female breast" (1916, p. 257). Abraham referred to this as a "cannibalistic impulse" (1916, p. 258).

In another case, Abraham (1916) treated a young man who, during the course of a delusional illness, had turned away from his fiancée. In the analysis the patient described a compulsive phantasy about eating excrement that was lying on the street. The patient then reported that since his childhood he had often had a craving for Johannes bread. When asked for associations with the Johannes bread, the patient recalled a childhood memory of a time when the road, near his home, was being dug up. The patient said the dirt on the road reminded him of excrement but it also glistened, which he likened to "mother-of-pearl". The patient had a further association which was a belief he had held as a child that the woman who lived across the road was a witch. Abraham noted the split between the "wicked witch" mother and the "mother-of-pearl". Abraham (1924) concluded that there was a "split" in the patient's mind; that beneath the sadistic or cannibalistic urges there existed a desire for a pleasurable or sucking activity. The idea that there was a split between a good mother and a bad mother was to prove persuasive later in the thinking of Klein, who seemed to follow through the implications of Abraham's investigations by arguing that the breast, in the mind of the infant, was also split between being a good object and a bad object.

Abraham concluded that the early oral stages in the development of the libido needed to differentiate between a biting and sucking phase. The first stage, characterized by the sucking impulse, was conceived to be pre-ambivalent and free from conflict. But later in the biting stage Abraham argued that ambivalence towards the object emerged whereby the impulse to incorporate or eat was replaced by an impulse to greedily destroy that which was perceived to be the source of food. We might say that Abraham was describing a sadistic infantile impulse of "biting the hand (or breast) that feeds", to coin a phrase. This theory was offered as a mental process which could account for "the grave conflicts which strike at the roots of his [the melancholic's] relation to his love-objects" (1924, p. 453). In other words Abraham observed his patients as unable to enjoy relationships, rather they were prone to damaging their chances of interpersonal fulfilment.

Finally Abraham noted in these cases that there was the occurrence of a special relationship or fixation to an isolated part of another person. Abraham described how the attacks at this stage of oral development were directed at only an isolated part of the body. He said he was reminded of the child who catches a fly, then cruelly pulls its leg off and then lets it go again. Of course this was an activity that Dr Seward had observed Renfeld doing while Renfeld was detained in the asylum. In her paper on "Weaning" (1936), Klein was most specific about the body part that merited attention, describing how the breast was the focus of early phantasies derived from the sensual pleasure of feeding. But she also observed sadistic and cannibalistic impulses directed at the breast and confirmed Abraham's earlier findings that the process of incorporation involved not only sucking but also biting. In "Some Reflections on the Oresteia", Klein (1963) argued that the act of killing mother was a symbolic attack on the breast. In the play, before Orestes kills his mother in revenge for the murder of his father Agamemnon, his mother pleads with him: "Would you strike at the breast that fed your milky gums?" Klein (1963) referred to this attack as a probable re-enactment of Orestes's original attack on his mother's breast as an infant and she cited Abraham's (1924) model of "vampire-like sucking" (p. 290) to illustrate the dynamic she was describing.

The count on the couch

As I begin to conclude here, I hope it has become apparent that Abraham's, and then Klein's ideas about a primitive infantile urge to suck and bite, are a possible explanation for the root of vampirism. In other words, the popularity of the idea of *Dracula* might be based on our profound identification with sucking and biting as it forms during our pre-memory infancy. In *Dracula* we have a rendering of the fundamental relationship between the infant's eye-contact with his mother during the earliest moments of feeding. Or more accurately we have a rendering of a damaged gaze. The count's piercing stare mesmerizes his victims before he gets his teeth into them. But his stare would seem to exemplify a deadly gaze, the antithesis of the loving gaze that is the normalizing feature of infant-mother bonding. The loving gaze, back and forth between mother and child, has been psychoanalytically conceived in terms of "mirroring" and is seen to be a prerequisite to healthy psychic development. Optic mirroring interplay begins during the time of early feeding and nurturance in the mother-infant dyad; the distance that the infant can see during its first weeks of life is ten to twelve inches which is naturally convenient inasmuch as it is the distance between the breast and the mother's eyes during feeding. The function of early mirroring in the psychic growth of the infant has a mediating function for the development of healthy outwardness in the infancy (Pines, 1984, 1985). However, as we know, Count Dracula is so bereft of a living self that his mirror image disappears altogether. Take the instance where Jonathan Harker is shaving in the morning following his arrival in Transylvania:

> Suddenly I felt a hand on my shoulder, and heard the Count's voice saying to me, "Good morning". I started, for it amazed me that I had not seen him, since the reflection of the glass covered the whole room behind me. In starting I had cut myself slightly, but did not notice it that moment. Having answered the Count's salutation, I turned to the glass again to see how I had been mistaken. This time there could be no error, for the man was close to me, and I could see him over my shoulder. But there was no reflection of him in the mirror! (p. 25).

The count is furious at Jonathon Harker's shaving mirror, vilifying it as "a foul bauble of man's vanity" (p. 26), and throws it out of the window whereupon it shatters into a thousand pieces. The soulless count is a parent without love, and his mirthless offspring, in the form of the three female vampires taunt him: "You yourself never loved; you never love!"

What we have in Stoker's vampire is the imago of a psychopathic wound; a man-mother-being unable to be reflected. Count Dracula's narcissistic fracture makes the ailment of the little boy Narcissus seem minor by comparison; at least the little boy Narcissus saw his reflection in the water. Dracula cannot see himself and this evokes the type of narcissistic disturbance that Heinz Kohut (1971) sees at the root of drug addiction. Kohut points to a formative disturbance or trauma in the process of early feeding where there is a deficiency in the shared gaze between mother and infant at the breast, largely arising from a defective maternal empathy. Kohut argues that the infant who is left for excessive periods in a state of hunger may grow up to use drugs as a replacement for the lost desired object (mother). *Dracula* would seem to exemplify those characteristics of addiction which Kohut describes as clinically extant.

So can we see drug use as a desire for greedy and desperate oral incorporation, that is intent on a revengeful and destructive attack on the object? I am reminded of the number of times injecting drug users have reported that they chew on the rubber bung of their needle—or teat as it is technically known—when they are craving, evoking the image of a hungry infant. Drug intoxication leads to acute appetite suppression and so when addicts talk about their "drug hunger" it would seem that the desire for actual food is replaced by drug food. *Dracula* depicts the nightmare turmoil of hunger and desire to the point of obsession. As a mirror to the dangerousness and deathliness of a life-risking abuse, the perversion of pleasure, and the gratuity of drug harm, *Dracula* conveys the loneliness and isolation of a life addicted, the dark abyss of the underworld of dealers and other addicts, the compulsion to damage, and absence of true loved ones. The addict's search for chemical solace is an attempt at finding love and comfort and it is the complete absence of these states that underpins the fate of Count Dracula.

Arthur's cure

The sense of helplessness in the reader/observer of the novel (in a sense we are Dr Seward) as Renfeld descends in madness, resembles the feeling one may often encounter when working with drug users. Many users defend their habits, describing their use as recreational or occasional, being blasé about their habit, while from the outside one can see the denial masking an inevitable collapse. It can be like watching a car crash in slow motion, the doomed sense of the inevitable and muffled futility of words. So what is to be done?

Getting across the threshold of denial is a common first step in many addiction programmes, including Alcoholics Anonymous and Narcotics Anonymous. *Dracula* provides something of a template for the challenge of meeting the spread of the drug pandemic. The sense of blood bonding and blood affiliation in the novel, aside from the immediate parallel of the drug injection, brings to mind also the journey of HIV as a defining outcome of the consequences of sharing and cross infection. Arthur's question about drug users' fascination in *Dracula* may be at its clearest in the resemblance of the plight of the maligned and blood diseased outsider. *Dracula* presses home the process of vilification: those who are addicts can be seen as vampires, much maligned, arguably treated with less dignity than a leper would have been a hundred years ago. Might we yet feel sympathy for Count Dracula who, as the offspring of the family of Dracul and Vlad the infamous impaler, appears to have a transgenerational history with an absence of good objects or good parental love. What disturbances lie at the root of his destructiveness?

So what was it that inspired Bram Stoker to such an eloquent portrayal of hungry infant turmoil? We do know that from the start for the infant Bram life was not all plain sailing. Leatherdale (1985) tells us that

> The first years of his life were taken up with no more than simple survival. He was bed-ridden for his first seven years. The cause or nature of this disorder has never been established, nor even hinted at with any confidence. In view of the complete recovery that Bram made, and the athletic feats that were to follow, it is plausible that the malady had its causes in his mind rather than his body (p. 58).

Stoker appears to have recovered better than his character. Count Dracula seems to signify the impossibility of recovery. But if we could help the count, what might be the course of action? Traditionally addiction treatment programmes aim to impact upon the recovery of the self. Poor self-image and low self-esteem can be superseded by experiences with peers, in group therapy and in individual therapy which bring about a more positive self-image. At Phoenix House, a concept residential treatment centre that used to be in South London, the recovery of the self-image was symbolized by a rather unusual treatment regime called "mirror therapy". Mirror therapy was initiated when a resident was felt by their peers to be avoiding important issues in their recovery. The group would prescribe the individual to sit in front of a mirror for up to two hours in order for them to take a good look at themselves. Such inward-looking treatment interventions have probably been rightly discarded in favour of the type of "outsight" or outward mirroring that is readily available in interpersonal therapy like group therapy (Pines, 1984). In treatment, the addict must face their problem self, their excitement and drug hunger, and especially examining their patterns of relating to others. In a sense the process of recovery is about re-creating the self and other in relationship. But this is not born out of self-examination, rather it is the reciprocity of self and other that is the start point for recovery. The base for a new lifestyle lies in the capacity for the client to begin to synthesize new sustaining relations. In the first place the new synthesis is experienced in treatment, with therapists and peers.

Psychotherapy with Count Dracula would be arduous and long I am sure; hundreds of years of transgenerational fragmentation and a splintered mirroring would need in-depth rebuilding. If we were to carry Abraham's work forward we would be interested in the impact of teething on psychic development, what is it like to develop the means to bite oneself and others, how is the pain managed, is the pain of teething the first real mind pain that is the basis for our search for pain relief in later life?

Arthur's theorem

A footnote to Arthur is needed here. It was he who set me off on the Transylvanian trail. After a couple of months in recovery, as I mentioned, Arthur developed an interest in photography. It was actually the beginning of what might be well described as exuberant scoptophilic recovery. His energies, which had been bludgeoned by his drug use became revitalized. Apart from setting off the fire detector once, the darkroom on the unit became a source of inspiration. He started developing striking visual images of the hospital, its grounds, and those around him. In his experiments he transposed negatives to form interesting overlays of people seemingly interacting. He made numerous self-portraits, and it was as if he was trying to locate his new self. He took to producing black and white images: this was cheaper, but arguably more effective. I remember he took some photographs of the grounds at the Bethlem after it had snowed. "Snow" was a street name for his favourite tipple, cocaine, so Arthur photographing real snow and creating some very interesting images seemed symbolic. He discovered a creative self in a world that had previously been lost or perhaps never truly founded. Like the count, Arthur had a dark room, but unlike the count, Arthur had a glimpse that light was good, and that sometimes day was better than night.

CHAPTER FOUR

The Prometheus Syndrome: addiction, death, and the liver in mind

A new syndrome?

Clients in therapy will often bring dreams to therapy of lost loved ones. In these dreams, damaged or dying people or objects appear to be resurrected. Though rather than this being a sign of self-repair and health gain, the resuscitation of a dead or dying object appears to result only in a further cycle of self-destruction. It was with the help of the late Henri Rey, who had previously described a similar clinical phenomenon (1994a), that I try to raise this clinical observation to a general psychological theory of addiction. Based on the Greek myth of Prometheus I propose a specific cycle of resurrection-wish which I call *the Prometheus Syndrome* (Winship, 1999). In brief, I have been struck by the similarities between the punishment cycle in the Greek myth of Prometheus and the deathly cycle of self-punishment in drug addiction. In particular the attack on Prometheus's liver in the myth seems apt because so often it is the liver of the addict which is assaulted in drug addiction. The biological process of detoxification in the liver, where toxic substances are rendered harmless and prepared for discharge, might be said to have a psychological counterpart whereby the detoxification of noxious and toxic mentalizations might be discharged in the process of therapy. This therapeutic task might be said to be a sort of psychic dialysis, where the therapist acts as a detoxifying agent.

This concept of deep organic mentation advances psychoanalytic theory beyond its traditional compartments. Historically psychoanalysis has been preoccupied with surface sensations: the body as ego in the first place; sensory and erogenous zones such as the mouth, and then skin as an object, and then other primary objects of early sensuality—mouth, ears, eyes, penis, vagina, and so forth. Bion said that the mind might be said to function as an internal bodily system: for instance, he said, the alimentary canal. I argue further that we might need to consider a more complex notion of "organ as ego"; and in this case the liver as a mental process. The question, as to how the development and function of bodily organs impacts upon emotional states, seeks deeper corrugations of psychobiology that might throw light on dangerous and destructive addictive urges.

Prometheus bound

Prometheus was the cousin of Zeus and assisted him in the overthrow of his father Cronus. Following the triumph, Cronus and the other Titans were banished to a gloomy abyss called Tartarus, deeper and darker than Hades. Presiding over the earth, Zeus wanted to utterly destroy mankind. However, Prometheus stood against the idea. Thus, it was decided that the mortals should instead share the resources of the world, and that the great ox would be divided with Prometheus arbitrating to determine which parts of the great ox would be eaten by mortals and which parts by the gods. Why Prometheus sought to deceive Zeus is not clear, but when Prometheus made up two pouches he covered one pouch in prime flesh which merely concealed bones, while the other ordinary pouch concealed the superior meat. Zeus, however, learned of Prometheus's ruse and selected the ox paunch that secured the superior meat for the gods. In order to punish Prometheus for his trickery Zeus deprived fire from mankind. But Prometheus ignored the prohibition and smuggled fire in a giant fennel stalk and made it a gift to mankind. In revenge Zeus ordered a more severe punishment; this time he had Prometheus restrained by Violence and Might, who shackled Prometheus to a rock. Aeschylus tells in his play of the great pain and terrible abuse that is heaped upon Prometheus including lightning and organ devouring beasts. Best known is the daily descent of an eagle which devours Prometheus's liver. Because Prometheus is a Titan, he cannot die, and each day his liver grows back, and each night the liver devouring punishment is repeated. This punishment carried on for an age until Zeus permits his son, Hephaestus, who had reluctantly made the shackles that held Prometheus, to unbind him.

The myth, memorable in its gruesomeness, has become embedded in our culture. Percy Bysshe Shelley tackled the myth in his play *Prometheus Unbound* which was published in about 1820. In the play Shelley used the drama to situate the triumphant unshackling of Prometheus as a political metaphor in which the power of the executive is overthrown, with Prometheus cast as a sort of messiah of the underclass who is heroically stoical in the face of the folly of gods. Percy's wife, Mary Shelley (1818), had already subtitled her novel *Frankenstein* as *A Tale of a Modern Prometheus*, positing that Dr Frankenstein's god-like creation of life, though monstrously scientific, could be seen as some equivalent to Prometheus giving life to man. Prometheus's temerity in giving fire to man against the will of Zeus is set along another axis by Mary Shelley, with Dr Frankenstein using electricity as the modern equivalent of fire to give life to his creation. The outcome for both Prometheus and the monster is ruinous, with both suffering for an age.

A century later, Freud's interest was captured particularly by Prometheus's act of fire theft. Freud interpreted the theft as symbolic of taking power away from the father, Zeus. It was an example of an enactment of the Oedipus complex (cf. Shengold, 1991). Freud points in particular to the fennel stalk in the myth of Prometheus which Freud refers to as a "penis tube" (1932, p. 289). It seems a reasonable supposition on Freud's part to argue that the myth of Prometheus represents a universal story about the struggle between fathers and sons. Prometheus stands for a state of combustion with authority; in the first place Prometheus is involved in the original patriarchal overthrow by aiding Zeus to kill his father Cronus, and then again Prometheus challenges the new authority of Zeus. Prometheus's acts of defiance are certainly heroic, though perhaps foolhardy. Prometheus is something of a trickster, and his act of trying to dupe Zeus with the ox pouches seems to place him unnecessarily in a precarious position. But Prometheus might be forgiven for his defiance of Zeus. He might have expected that after the overthrow of the dictator Cronus there would have been a new democratic order whereby the younger generation of gods would have desired and seen through a new social and political order on Olympus.

Instead Zeus executes no democratic pact of goodwill and fairness, rather he simply installs himself as a new sovereign tyrannical patriarch who takes an even more stern position with the mortals. Confronted with yet another tyranny ruling over mother earth, Prometheus acts defiantly and bravely on behalf of mankind.

Freud's Oedipal rendering of the myth seems more than well enough placed then. However, there are further aspects of the myth which merit attention. For instance, the split of the good food and the bad food when the great ox is divided up, bring to mind a pre-Oedipal drama where the infant perceives mother to be either good or bad; the oral stage split, as I discussed in the previous chapter, that Karl Abraham suggested was more indicative of the infant-child's relation to the mother. And whereas Freud left the myth at the point of Oedipal overthrow (the gift of fire), when we follow the myth through to its climax where Prometheus is tethered in perpetuity, then some other dynamic features come into focus. The nocturnal attack of the eagle is a motif of death that has some echoes of *Dracula* where the idea of eternal death is a compelling hinge of the narrative. Prometheus becomes an imago of a universal nightmare: the prospect of an eternal living death, or hell as it is known in Christian mythology. We feel sympathetic towards Prometheus because in contrast to Zeus, Prometheus appears to have benign intentions towards mankind. Prometheus is revered for saving mankind through his gift of fire. His suffering therefore touches us as a selfless act of sacrifice. The punishment where his side is gouged resembles the fate of Jesus Christ on the cross, whose side, as it is told in the Bible, was lanced by a Roman guard. Indeed, as Christ was shackled and killed for attempting to "save" mankind, we can therefore see Prometheus as a forerunner to the messianic hero who suffers on behalf of man. Given that both the Greeks and Christians constructed myths that involved a grisly sacrifice of their god-messiah, one might wonder about some unfortunate inherent disposition towards a sort of culture of sadism as the functional basis for knitting society together.

But setting aside these rather wide-ranging cultural and political questions, we might wonder why it is that Prometheus's liver is so specifically subject to the repeated attacks in the myth? Why not some other body part? Firstly we might say that the attack on the liver is a talion punishment insofar as it is the largest gland in the body, hugely metabolic and therefore an anatomical seat of warmth, or bodily fire. That is to say, Prometheus steals fire from the gods and therefore suffers the deprivation of his own internal fire. The cycle of punishment is repeated because the liver regrows overnight. Indeed, the liver is the only organ tissue in the body which is capable of regeneration. Dr Adrian Bomford, a liver expert at the world renowned Liver Unit at Kings College Hospital, London, believes that the fact of liver regeneration may have been known to early Greek physicians (Bomford, 1998). Though he does not know of any scholarly research which supports this supposition he believes that early Greek physicians may well have observed the regenerating capabilities of the liver during their experiments on animals. Although the biological detoxifying function of the liver may not have been understood by Greek physicians, it is intriguing that Prometheus is cast as a sort of cleansing agent, that is to say the toxic attack on mankind by Zeus where he seeks total annihilation is ameliorated by Prometheus's compassion. The fire in the fennel stalk not only appears as symbolic in terms of its life- saving properties but also in terms of fire as a cleanser. Casting Prometheus's liver in this role in the myth suggests that the early Greek physicians may have been intuitively aware of the function of the liver.

The liver in mind

What has this got to do with addiction then? It should be clear by now that I am suggesting that the particular attack on the liver in the case of Prometheus is a repeated act, a cyclical occurrence of death-life-death-life. The myth is of particular interest because in the context of alcohol and drug use, liver damage is one of the most serious consequences of chronic addiction. Although liver damage occurs directly as a result of alcohol use, other drug use can cause damage to the liver indirectly. For instance, among injecting drug users septic techniques and sharing dirty injecting equipment have led to an epidemic of hepatitis, a viral infection which attacks liver functioning, detectable in more than 50 per cent of injecting drug users in some regions (Smith et al., 1992). The second reason the physiological function of the liver is of interest is because becoming "clean" following addiction involves a physical process of detoxification. The liver's physiological function, as the most efficient organ of detoxification, is well known. But that it might have a psychological counterpart is the subject of my further inquiry. The notion that we might parallel biological processes as a descriptor for considering mental process is not without precedent.

For instance W. R. Bion (1967, 1970) described mental process in terms of the alimentary canal, where he talked about "food for thought", and referred to the way that we "digested ideas", and so on. I consider here if there is a protomental counterpart to the powerful detoxifying function of the liver with case illustrations.

Brian

Brian was a 32-year-old injecting drug user who suffered from a blood disorder arising from liver damage caused by his drug use. I worked with him over three admissions for inpatient treatment and then in follow-up in two years of outpatient work. Over this period he was admitted to hospital on several occasions to treat his potentially life-threatening liver condition. He was at a loss as to why he could not stop. Even though he knew the life-threatening consequences of his continued drug use, he seemed compelled to take drugs. He described himself as having a death wish. It was hard not to agree. During his third admission to the inpatient drug unit in as many years, he began to recount some early recollections. In one of these recollections, he spoke of a time when as a child he used to love going swimming at the local public baths. When he was eleven years old, a child drowned in the pool one day. The account of the death that Brian and his friends either heard or constructed was that the child had drowned when his hand had got stuck in the grill at the bottom of the deep end of the pool. It perhaps matters less whether this was true or not, but the following week Brian went to the pool as usual and, without really thinking, dived into the deep end of the pool and swam down to the bottom whereupon he poked his fingers through the same grill bar which had trapped the hand of the child the week before. Brian said he knew it was "wrong" and "dangerous", but he just "had see what would happen".

Recounting this event, some twenty or so years later, Brian said he still felt a "sickly thrill". The act of revisiting the point of death, the bottom of the pool, seemed to be indicative of some nascent morbid compulsion. He repeated the act because he felt compelled to do so, not knowing why. Death became an actual external place which perhaps mirrored an inner mental space to which he was drawn to risk danger or even death. The grill, an enticing object in this space, signified an object that was perversely thrilling. Death became a filial matter of sensation/no-sensation perhaps. In adulthood, this dangerous thrill-seeking urge had become a compulsion as Brian risked his life taking mind-altering substances. Instead of poking his fingers into the grill, he poked needles into himself until his flesh had begun to resemble the rusty grate at the bottom of the pool, the infectious source of his liver damage.

Another of his recollections provided further material about his early mental life. Recorded verbatim by his key worker, Brian reported: "I'm four years old. I'm in my grandparent's house. In the front room my grandmother has an oil heater of some kind, shaped like a stool. I sit on it with no clothes on. There is excruciating pain as I sit on the heater because I thought it was a stool. My mother is in the next room. She runs in and cuddles me." The recollection suggested a moment of blinding pain, a moment where all thought is extinguished. In some ways this blind pain has echoes of the point of death in the swimming pool recollection, the annihilation of thinking. This tendency to obliterate all thought would seem to be part of the motivation to use drugs, the retreat from reality that leads to unconsciousness.

The experience of working with Brian often felt like he was paying lip service to what you were saying, as if one's best intentions were being extinguished. When Brian went home for his first weekend leave after several months of drug-free rehabilitation as an inpatient, he began using drugs almost at the first opportunity, obliterating several months of therapeutic work. This relapse was repeated on each occasion after inpatient treatment. It was as if he came into treatment for a detoxification as a temporary respite. In the end we were not able to reach Brian. The addictive attachment to the drug of object choice needs to undergo a transition to an attachment to the therapist. It would seem that this shift never adequately took place in Brian's case. In his case he seemed to prefer to be attached to death, rather than to the life-giving potential of therapists and recovering peers.

Daniel

As well as his poly drug misuse 28-year-old Daniel had an appetite for home-made fireworks. During an admission on the inpatient unit he made such a large firework that when he let it off, it was heard a mile or so away by one of the unit staff who was at home. Daniel had an explosive personality. He was bitterly disappointed with the world around him. He had enjoyed some fame as a child celebrity, but this had not translated into success in adulthood. After setting the firework off, he was discharged from the unit. He had made some steps towards sustained sobriety during his admission, and I think he had found the idea of recovery to be one of the few things to hold his attention since his teens. I saw him for eighteen months on a twice weekly basis as an outpatient. But my experience of working with him was disorientating. I was never sure that I existed in Daniel's mind. He would say he saw me as a "blank screen" or a "sounding board", and that he liked the opportunity to talk to me, to get things off his chest. I did indeed seem to be blanked out by him.

Daniel would come into sessions and talk about his turbulent relationships, both at work and socially. His life always seemed to be full of drama, at least on the surface. I was never sure if this was real, or if somehow he felt that he had to entertain me. It was as if the brinkmanship of his drug lifestyle seemed to have shifted from opiates to relationships. The latter seemed somewhat healthier. On occasions he would say he experienced his therapy as "mundane" or "irrel-evant". He viewed me disdainfully as if I were a flat blank board, empty. Despite my efforts, there were only a few occasions when he seemed interested in what I thought or might say. He seemed to want me to bounce back his thoughts untransformed. He had a superior air about him and even after two years there was little rapport or warm feeling. When therapy came to a close, he was still drug free, but I was not sure that I really knew him still. At our last session Daniel gave me a book about warplanes. He said he didn't know what I liked so he'd bought something he liked. The book was so far from my taste that it confirmed how little of the space between him and me had been bridged.

Two years later I saw him again for a review appointment. He had been using heavily for several months and his life had been plagued by further failed relationships and loss of work. When we met, I was struck that there was little in the way of a feeling of connection between us. Not that this was particularly surprising. He was angry and frustrated, but I am not sure I recognized just how furious he was. Two weeks later he killed himself. In the coroner's court we heard that he had killed himself in his bathroom and that the walls and ceiling were sprayed with blood. He left a suicide note that accused me and our service of neglect. The young community worker Daniel had been seeing felt so distressed by all the events that she left the profession. There seemed to be an obliteration of the potential of the professional thinking other.

The dead thinking other

The process of shifting addictive attachments is necessary in helping clients remain drug free when they leave the security of the treatment setting. Clients need to be able to hold their therapist in mind away from the treatment unit or psychotherapy session (cf. Winship & Unwin, 1997). Balint refers to the possibility that the client might become addicted to their therapy. Addicts in recovery who attend Narcotics Anonymous (NA) or Alcoholics Anonymous (AA) sometimes talk about going through a phase of being addicted to the group. This may well be the case for people with addictive personalities: when they cease one addiction they replace it with another. However, addiction to a group or a therapist would seem an altogether healthy step in the right direction; dependency on good enough relationships, or groups of relationships would constitute a level of normalizing well-being towards an independent capacity to remain drug free.

In the cases of Daniel and Brian there did not appear to be an adequate internalization of the therapy or the therapist in order to maintain a drug-free state. I certainly would not say in either case they became "addicted" to their therapy. It was rather more that they "suffered" their therapy; they went through the steps of therapy almost on the way back to relapse. Their cases might at first seem somewhat self-defeating scenarios to choose in order to illustrate the process of psychoanalytic therapy. Indeed, they might appear to offer anti-evidence as to the effectiveness therapy. However, worst case scenarios can sometimes offer helpful veins of learning. There is certainly less depth to the case presentations than one would perhaps like to see, though in each case there is evidence of the salient dynamic, whereby behaviour appears to be an urge towards flirtation with death. Both cases chime with Betty Joseph's idea about addiction to near death experiences. Brian's repetition of diving to the bottom of the pool seemed to be a precursor totouching death with drug use later in life, and Daniel's dalliance with fireworks suggested a dangerous appetite for explosives.

Apart from the blinding pain, what is striking about Brian's second early recollection, when he sat on the heater, is the absence of his mother. Although in the recollection his mother returns to cuddle him, during the course of his therapy it became clear that Brian was unfamiliar with being contained by the thinking other. His mother was initially idealized although later he recalled how he returned home from school one day (at eight years) to find his puppy had been given away without warning because it was defecating on the carpet. For both Brian and Daniel, the repetitious use of substances were attempts to numb mental pain, a retreat from reality and perhaps an attempt to return to a state of nothingness: that is to say opiate narcosis numbing mental pain with a sort of sleep death urge; the word morphine deriving from Morpheus, god of sleep.

In the foregoing case accounts we might hypothesize that there was an absence of an adequate, or good enough thinking other, indeed the thinking other has the hue of a barely alive or even dead object. It is of particular interest here that Henri Rey argued that the creation of sensation in drug use is one way of attempting to bring alive internal objects that are felt to be dead or dying. According to Rey, where there is an inner state of "deadness, there is a search for stimulants and production of sensory experience by means of alcohol, drugs, hashish, cutting, perversions, promiscuity" (1994, p. 9). Internal objects that are felt to be motionless are perceived to be excited by sensation, thus the drug user activates the inner dead world by chemical sensori-motor activity. Rey notes that there is a type of "virtual energy" which is activated in drug use whereby a phantasy of aliveness, comparable to the kind of mental activity that occurs during dreaming.

Patients who are in the early stage of recovery allude to these deathly inner states, for example describing feeling like "death warmed up" during the recovery phase post-withdrawal. Spontaneous withdrawal from an addictive drug is called "cold turkey", referring to the piloerection occurring during the bodily shivers when the flesh resembles the skin of a dead turkey. Drug addiction itself is often described as a "living death". Rey (1994a, 1994b) has discussed how certain psychic manoeuvres are employed to keep alive internal objects perceived to be damaged or dying. He argues that damaged good objects are continually resuscitated in order that they might be put right through a process of reparation. In reflecting on Freud's (1917) theory of identification with the dead loved ones inside, Rey argues that identification with the lost loved one may be for reasons of reparation as well as guilt:

> In *Mourning and Melancholia* Freud made the great discovery of the identification of the lost external object with the ego of the subject, and the continuation of the attacks on the object by the melancholic by attacking himself with self recriminations. I suggest that the object was thus kept alive by identification for reasons other than guilt alone, that is, for the sake of being able to carry on reparation as well Rey, (1994, p. 236).

Patients bring these dead or dying objects to therapy because they do not know how to repair them themselves. Rey makes a distinction between the process of identificatory reparation and the pathological rumination where there is a failure to make reparation. In the first instance the object is resurrected in order to keep it alive so that it might be repaired, in the second instance the object is kept alive for the purpose of self-persecution or guilt, a difference between depressive position reparation and schizoid or manic reparation. Rey (1994) cites the case of a woman who became obsessed with her kidney which had suffered a minor infection following a pregnancy. The patient underwent a great number of fruitless investigations. As if ruminating over her kidney fearing it was irreparably damaged, she appeared to reproduce the pain and worry in a way that suggested that she was unable to allow her kidney to be well. During the analysis Rey found that the patient associated her kidney with her mother: the damaged kidney had become a condensation of her mother and the damage the patient thought she had done to her mother when she was a baby. In her bringing her kidney to analysis, Rey discovered that it was in fact her relationship with her mother that was in need of reparation.

In a similar case I saw a patient who was tortured by facing the recurring loss of her father. She was a 60-year-old woman with diabetes who had a long history of depression and life-limiting obesity. She described herself as "addicted to chocolate". She said that she could not stop eating chocolate even though she knew she was "eating herself to death". She had been told by the diabetic clinic that her excessive sugar intake had caused damage to her liver functioning and that continued consumption of chocolate was potentially life threatening. When she said that this addictive appetite had been with her since childhood I asked her what her childhood had been like. She told me that when she was three years old her father had been lost at sea during the Second World War while on active service. She said that it did not begin to dawn on her until she was about eight years old that she did not have a daddy like her friends. As she walked home from school around this time there was a flag pole in view beyond the houses where she lived. Every day she would look at the pole and think it was her father's ship trying to get home. Some time later she told me about the trauma of a stillbirth when she was twenty-five years old (the approximate age of her father at death). After the birth she said that she did not get to hold her daughter. There had been no funeral for her daughter. She then said that for years afterwards she had a recurring dream in which she was giving birth and saying to the midwife: "Don't let my baby die, I've had eleven stillbirths." She did not know why there were eleven stillbirths in the dream. It appeared that in her unconscious she had not endured just one stillbirth, but many. Over and over again she had re-experienced the trauma of the birth, perhaps in the same way that she had tortured herself looking at the flag pole, representing her father, wishing for his return. Not knowing where her daughter had been cremated re-invoked the loss of her father whose body had never been found. Her lifetime addiction to chocolate appeared to be an ongoing effort to fill the emptiness and loss that she felt inside. When she spoke about chocolate she did so in an excited way, as if the deadness could be dispersed and replaced by something alive.

It could be argued that there was an impossibility of mourning a stillbirth, although the normal deep grieving had turned into a self-destructive compulsion as a result of the conflation of the earlier loss of her father. Rey impresses upon us that it is not whole figures that are the focus of pathogenic process mourning; for instance, in the case of his kidney patient, the bodily organ had become what might be described as a screen object coding a tangled psychopathology with a somatic representation. Likewise, with the client addicted to chocolate, the substance was phantasized as having rejuvenating powers; the chocolate was a screen object which concealed the underlying trauma and damage. There was no space for reparation or acceptance, instead, death and damage were continually revisited in a self-tormenting way.

Discussion

This recycling of death and damage is perhaps more universal than we might expect. Returning to the myth of Prometheus, I suggest a provisional formulation concerned with the concurrent factors in the case material: that the pathological process of revisiting the dead and damaged objects or space inside is symbolically equated with the repetitious self-damage of drug use. This is a preliminary assertion that may be the basis of developing a specific object relational schema for drug addictive behaviour.

In the initial stages of recovery from addiction the therapist needs to become a new synthesis of an alive and awake thinking other, alert to reality and capable of enduring mental pain. The idea of "a thinking other" has a particular lineage in psychoanalytic theory and practice. The process of thinking by proxy for the infant is a biological necessity in the first place; the infant cannot manage to organize their thoughts adequately enough to self-care, but it is also a psychological necessity because the infant cannot manage feelings of anxiety and distress. The thinking mother needs to soothe, before the infant can develop a capacity for self-soothing. Bion (1970) points out that protomental activity emerges as a concomitant of the developing cortex, the inorganic space that is filled by experience. The earliest moments of thinking emerge from sensation, either inter-sensual (from external sources) or intra-sensual (the emerging sensation of bodily function). These sensations and experiences provide a protomental template whereby biological and psychological processes weave together.

In the same way that Bion describes that there is a need for a thinking other in order to digest formative experiences of confusion and anxiety—a thinking process which he suggests is akin to the function of the alimentary canal, digesting thoughts and so on—I suggest that there is a far more active and powerful process of digestion that might need to operate in order to digest thoughts and experiences which are rather more toxic than normative. In order to detoxify noxious experiences, the work of the thinking other may be closer to the function of the liver rather than the alimentary canal. The liver in this sense is more active than Rey's idea of screen object: I suggest there is an actual psychobiological interweave. Bion describes that the thinking other in the first place is the mother and that the therapist re-enacts this function to some extent with the patient. The same might be said of the process of detoxifying toxic "psychomatter" that the patient brings to therapy.

The patients I have seen with severe and chronic addictions have endured life events which are more than the run-of-the-mill human suffering. That which these patients have brought to therapy, like so many patients who suffer from dangerous repetition compulsion disorders, have been noxious experiences which seem to be revisited time and time again. Like the continual repetitious attack in the Promethean legend, it would appear that the patients I have seen with chronic addictions have not been able to detoxify their experiences. Is it possible that the therapeutic process in these cases features a process of metabolization in the mind of the therapist? Rey (1998, personal communication) has alluded to a process of discharging or excreting thoughts in the formation of a healthy personality. In other words, Rey suggests that some thoughts can be discharged much in the same way that the body discharges toxic waste on a daily basis. Is it possible that the toxic experiences which are brought to therapy can be absorbed by the therapist and then not necessarily reflected back? Does the therapist have a function in enabling the healthy discharge of toxic experience? Perhaps there is waste matter of experience that is unnecessary or even dangerous to the healthy functioning of the organism. A mental discharge process is therefore required if the dynamic act of de-identification with the dead, dying, or noxious objects is to take place. The patient's previous toxic experiences are replaced by the real "tonic" experience of good enough therapy and the professional interest of the therapist.

In a sense then, the therapist is acting as a functioning organ of detoxification not unlike the liver. This function may be transitory if the patient is able to internalize enough of the therapist in order to carry out this function independently later. For some patients the detoxifying properties of psychotherapy may be required only in the short term where major life changes are achieved and sustained by the patient, with only brief intervention. For other patients however, exploratory therapy may need to be more intensive—residential for instance—where significant psychic and personality change is required; the equivalent, say, of an organ transplant. And finally, for patients who do not have the capacity for self-sufficient functioning beyond therapy, their chronic addictive urges mean that they require regular long-term therapeutic dialysis.

Drug addiction is characterized by repeated acts of masochism. These sadistic attacks do not necessarily arise from consciousness, indeed many addicts are perplexed by the idea that their drug use is driven by a self-destructive motivation. Instead they say they take drugs for pleasure or just to help them feel "normal". However, during the course of exploratory talking therapy self-annihilation tendencies become apparent in the memories, dreams, and imaginings of the patient.

The destructive forces at play can be said to be exerting "unconscious" disturbance and it is by tapping into these unconscious dynamics that the addictive urge can be understood. It is through the alteration of the patient's unconscious that addiction can be relieved. When addicts cease using it happens not as a result of a conscious decision to abstain, but rather some other ineffable force or factor that leads to a deeper level of will power, a will to unconscious power we might say.

By dint of rounding off, I just want to finish with Shelley's epilogue in *Prometheus Unbound* which conveys some of the essence of recovery, striking at the dark and overwhelming hold of addiction, where love and hope might at last triumph:

> To suffer woes which Hope thinks infinite;
> To forgive wrongs darker than death or night;
> To defy Power, which seems omnipotent;
> To love, and bear; to hope till Hope creates
> From its own wreck the thing it contemplates;
> Neither to change, nor falter, nor repent;
> This, like thy glory, Titan, is to be
> Good, great and joyous, beautiful and free;
> This is alone Life, Joy, Empire, and Victory

(1820, lines 570–578)P

CHAPTER FIVE

The pleasure paradox: nirvana and death dependency

Scope

In the chapter on milk and creation myths I attempted to show that there is a dynamic fusion that unconsciously connects birth, destruction, and intoxication. I then tried to discern how we might understand this fusion in terms of craving and addictive appetites. In proposing a specific syndrome, based on the myth of Prometheus, I drew attention to the way in which the psychological intricacies of drug ingestion might be seen to bind together at the point where the creation of euphoric mental states hovers close to a repeating urge towards death. In this chapter I develop the idea further with a theory that I call the "pleasure paradox", where I try to show how the pleasurable effects of a mind-altering act such as drug ingestion might run a close parallel with its dangerous consequences. Although my focus is on substance abuse, I would say that the idea of the "pleasure paradox" might meaningfully be applied to other compulsive acts of self-harm, such as cutting, vomiting, overeating, gambling, and other addictions where indulgence or overindulgence in the pleasure from an act brings about potentially deleterious consequences. My thesis is that at the very nub of the pleasure paradox there is a life and death struggle, a battle between Eros and Thanatos for the supremacy of the soul.

Attempts to modify compulsive behaviours fall short of addressing the submerged motivations towards self-destructivity. A deeply felt lack of pleasure or anhedonia is described by many addicts. Self-harming young people may also appear to experience life similarly, for instance describing boredom as a reason for cutting. The subsequent hedonistic search for pleasure, and even cutting can be pleasurable, appears to be an attempt to retreat from reality. Freud speculated that we were inclined to search for the blissful in-utero state that we once enjoyed, and that this urge was innate and universal. He called it the "nirvana principle", an escape to an earlier life stage where pleasure pre-dated consciousness. For some people, this search for nirvana can be occasional, for others it may become dangerously compelling, where ever more elaborate sado-masochistic behaviours aredeployed to bring about a desired state of bliss. In worst case scenarios, this urge towards pleasure might even be an attempt to vitalize a state of pleasure that has never really formed at all. The process of therapy is characterized by a shift from pleasure seeking to relationship seeking, where reality is embraced and not escaped.

Smoking kills

Several months into twice-weekly outpatient psychotherapy, one of my patients, a woman in her mid-twenties, told me she had given up smoking. The news initially passed me by, and it was only some months later that I thought about it. When I reflected on my lack of response, I wondered whether it was because she delivered the information in a rather matter-of-fact manner, as if it was not that important. I wondered whether my lack of response was a reflection of her complacency. But actually, I had no reason to assume she was complacent. It occurred to me that the news might have passed me by because I had more pressing concerns with her, with regard to that fact that she had, at least until lately, been fairly set on the idea that she was going to kill herself. After several months of twice-weekly psychotherapy, quitting smoking seemed less consequential than the fact that she was no longer feeling suicidal.

Of course hindsight is a great thing and, on reflection, I understood that there would be a link between smoking cessation and the diminishment of her suicidal feelings. That is to say, smoking was a symptom of her self-destructiveness and suicidality, albeit that smoking was expressed as an act as pleasurable or soothing. Her decision to stop smoking was therefore part of a deeper psychological shift towards life affirmation. In her battle between the love of life or Eros, and the love of death or Thanatos, it appeared that Eros had gained the upper hand. We know that Thanatos can be outwitted: Hesiod tells the story of how King Sisyphus twice outwitted Thanatos and his twin brother Hypnos (sleep), when it was his time to die. So how was it that my patient had come to give up smoking?

What had I done to help, or indeed had I done anything at all? At first glance at least it seemed that apart from making a note in her initial assessment that she smoked, the topic had never featured in our work together. And given the fact that smoking was rarely if ever spoken about in any of our sessions, it is at least a possibility that *not* talking about her habit had somehow had a paradoxical effect. The idea of paradoxical injunction has well-known currency in therapy. In marital therapy where couples present with sexual problems the therapist may begin by suggesting that the couples cease any sexual relations. The authoritative embargo seems to have a speedy effect in some cases when the couple find the sexual prohibition excites their desire for intimacy: a reverse outcome if you like. So was there a paradoxical effect of not talking about smoking with my client?

I think probably not. Instead, we talked about a tangled weave of life trajectories, her absent father, and the divorce of her parents when she was a young teen, her jealousy of her father's new girlfriend, and then the discovery that for several years before the divorce her father had been involved in a string of affairs. It was difficult to know whether she was more furious with his deceit or whether it was her mother's complacency that she really despised. Although she survived the worst effects of this emotional upheaval with occasional bouts of feeling like killing herself during her adolescence and had settled into a good professional career after university, when her boyfriend broke off their relationship all the old feelings came flooding back. She became suicidal, was prescribed anti-depressants, and referred to psychotherapy. She did cease taking anti-depressants during therapy too; this was planned, and I do not think her use of anti-depressants was compulsive, as can be the case, but rather for my client they seemed more a symptom of her general practitioner's anxiety.

Of course there was no paradoxical injunction in the case of my client that brought about smoking cessation. For it to be a proper intervention I would have needed to tell her to continue smoking. Nonetheless, the fact remains that we had not talked about smoking. I was interested enough to audit my most recent case load, at the time of sixteen clients, all of whom had been referred to the NHS for outpatient psychotherapy. I noticed that out of fourteen smokers at the start of therapy the majority had actually quit smoking during the course of their therapy. It had rarely been an issue of any significance, so the question as to what did happen to change their self-destructiveness came into focus. In each case, like the case described above, therapy was an opportunity to explore relationships, past and present; to examine feelings and experiences in regard to family, friends, colleagues, peers, and so forth. And finally, therapy was an opportunity to explore "then and there feelings" in the "here and now", in a transitional relationship with their therapist.

In treating addicts of illicit substances I have come to understand that telling drug users "not to take drugs" is futile. Indeed, it may even have the opposite effect. The idea of a campaign which runs "Smoking kills" might unwittingly be the best advertising a tobacco company could ask for. "Smoking kills" appeals to the unconscious allure of death that might be at the core of the appetite to smoke. Talking to addicts about the dangers of drug use is ineffective, and may even *increase* the likelihood that some users will take drugs. We might do well to start from an axiom that drug users take drugs because they *are* dangerous. It is one of the problems with "health education", where the aim is to discourage drug use, which begins with a sort of aversion therapy approach.

The dangers of misguided health education messages was apparent in a 2006 advertising campaign in Scotland where a television advert was broadcast on several occasions during the early weeks of August. I was in Edinburgh for the festival and I surmised that the advert was meant to coincide with the festival, and was therefore targeting young people in their early twenties who might be tempted to take heroin. In the advert a man was shown seated on a chair inhaling smoke rising from a square of silver foil. When the man reclined in a state of intoxication, various objects in the room, including the television, video, music player, and so forth began to disappear. In the end the man was left seated in a rather sparse environment. The intended message seemed clear enough: if you use drugs you will sell your belongings to pay for your habit. But given that at the beginning the flat looked messy and cluttered, by the time goods had disappeared the space began to look rather more habitable. Bad enough was the fact that the advert was instructive about how to smoke heroin—by showing us how to "chase the Dragon" (smoking heroin from the foil)—worse still was the suggestion that the clutter in your life could be dispersed by heroin. It was dangerously seductive, a sort of anti-kitsch ergonomic fashion statement on the creation of new urban living spaces. And to top it all off, the intoxicated repose of the user in the advert may have suggested a blissful sleepy state or Hypnos that might have appealed to people over-burdened by the strains of modernity. All in all, this was an expensive advert that may have done much more to sell heroin than to deter the market.

Perhaps we should begin by facing the possibility that engaging with drug users about the dangerousness of their drug use may appeal to their appetite for the alluring brinkmanship of life and death. This is Betty Joseph's (1982) thesis, that people can become addicted to death. She is less interested in their chosen compulsions which could be drugs, gambling, overeating, overwork, and so on, but rather she notes the common objective whereby death seems to have a certain allure. Nonetheless, we have seen an entire health industry and profession emerging over the last two decades which has predominantly been concerned with an aversion paradigm of approach that seeks to scare people away from drugs. Clearly it has not worked. There is a question as to whether we should be talking about drugs at all, either in prevention campaigns or in treatment.

The idea that we might not talk about drugs, as it was in the cases where I did not talk about smoking and yet smoking cessation was a clinical outcome, is at least a worthwhile hypothesis. Over the last thirty years, we have seen a drug treatment industry which seems intent on keeping the drug itself at the very centre of the conversation. I am thinking about the philosophy of harm-minimization programmes where dose stabilization and maintenance prescribing has been one of backbones of health education. I have lost count of the thousands of hours I have spent in micro negotiations with addicts about what their stabilization dose should be. It seems to me that the direction of harm minimization has been largely futile. With the ever continuing escalation of drug use, we must conclude that the philosophy of health education has been massively ineffective in curbing the spread of the drug epidemic.

So what should we be talking about with our addicted clients? Drug users are only too keen to talk about their dangerous drug habit. Getting addicts to talk about anything else other than drugs, like feelings or relationships, is the challenge. The simple "not talking about" theorem of the smoking cure in my audited cases belies the more arduous task of contemplating the other things that need to be talked about. But herein lies the rub; how do you get addicts to talk about something else?

"Drug talk" is second only in popularity to talk about "stopping". The same might be said about talking about dieting for people who have compulsive food appetites, that is to say, much more time is spent talking about dieting than dieting itself. A good example of the addict talking about his habit is J. M. Barrie's (1928) collection of smoking stories in *My Lady Nicotine*. The book portrays the way in which the smoker savours his nicotine but also the minutiae of detail associated in discussing the habitual activities and paraphernalia of the committed smoker. Barrie illustrates how he and his friends especially like to talk about the "evils" of smoking, and how they should stop. But instead of stopping, talking about nicotine became a compulsive activity that fuels the urge to smoke rather than rescinding it.

Perhaps the difficulty of getting drug users to talk about feelings starts to account for the fact that many psychotherapists are reluctant to see drug users. It has always been something of an anathema that many psychotherapists, including those working in the NHS, have said that they will not see an addict until they have been "clean" for two years. In the space vacated by psychotherapists it appears that behaviour therapists have occasionally entered the fray. The work of behaviour therapy from the mid 1970s onwards has promised to offer quick and cheap solutions to a whole raft of mental health problems, including drug addiction. For instance, there have been experiments with "cue exposure" for addiction. Cue exposure has been found to be valuable in the treatment of some anxiety conditions and some phobias and compulsions too. For example, in the treatment of a spider phobia the therapist uses a technique of gradual "exposure" to the spider (the cue), firstly getting the patient to look at pictures of a spider before looking at real spiders in a jar for instance, and then after some weeks of preparation the client will touch the spider and hereupon the client is cured. Having worked for some time on Isaac Marks's unit at the Bethlem and Maudsley hospital, I have seen this "cue exposure" method applied to all manner of obsessive and anxiety disorders from psychotic delusions to paedophilia.

The wide acclaim for the method of behaviour therapy in the 1970s and early 1980s lent impetus to a trial where a behavioural approach was applied to treating drug users. The experiment involved re-trying the cue exposure method, with a similar set of premises as the spider phobia programme. I was working on the inpatient drug dependency unit at the Bethlem Royal Hospital in 1981 where the programme was trialled. The programme was planned to run over six week and went like this: over the first two weeks the client was shown pictures of drugs and asked to rate levels of anxiety and excitation which were monitored and recorded by the research psychologist on each occasion before, during, and after the exposure. For example, the client was asked to look at a picture of drugs and asked to talk about feelings, and this was maintained until the anxiety and craving had diminished. These sessions were repeated with increasing exposure to the patient's drug of choice over weeks three and four, touching pictures and then actual assorted paraphernalia like spoons, needles, and so forth. The real drug (or a mimic powder) was finally introduced, with the patient looking and touching the drug.

The programme culminated in the research psychologist leaving the patient alone in the room with the drug. The aim was the hope that the simulation of a real-time exposure would mean that the client would not experience a level of urge to use, and would therefore be able to desist from taking the drug. The longer-term aim was that this would be good preparation for non laboratory conditions after discharge.

One of the first cue exposure subjects was Richard. Richard seemed much younger than his twenty years, prone to bad-tempered outbursts and even head-banging when things became difficult. He had a difficult time with the other residents on the unit and did not seem to be able to fit in with them at all. The fact that Richard had been mostly addicted to cough mixture did not endear himself with his peers who rather treated him as "not a real addict". When Richard volunteered to do the cue exposure programme, it was not clear to many of us that he had had much of a problem with heroin at all, despite his claims to the contrary. Nonetheless, he was recruited by the psychology research team and he took to the cue exposure programme rather enthusiastically. Richard enjoyed his individual time with the psychologist; perhaps he was made to feel that engaging in an innovative new programme of therapy was going to be the answer to how best to treat drug users. The sessions gave Richard something to talk about in group sessions, as he fed back the detail of the exposure programme to other residents. The sessions with the psychologist ran to plan, step by step, pictures, paraphernalia, talking about craving, and so on. After the six week stepped programme came the session when Richard would be exposed to the drug, and be left in the lab on his own. Amid great anticipation, Richard soon returned to the ward with his face dappled in powder, grinning like a kid who had just dipped his head in a packet of sherbet.

In spite of our disappointment, not all seemed to have been lost, because while the cue exposure may have failed, Richard's act of delinquency met with a hearty degree of approval among his fellow patients. Possibly for the first time in his life, Richard seemed to experience some sense of what it was to be accepted as "one of us". I think I understood that there is one thing worse than being a member of an anti-group, and that not being a member of any group. The cue exposure programme continued for a short while afterwards, but soon died away. I am not sure it can be said to be entirely assigned to a place of embarrassing archival interest in the history of psychiatry, along with bloodletting and brain surgery, because some of these methods are prone to coming in and out of fashion. To be fair, further studies finally proved that the extra effort (and not inconsiderable expense) of cognitive behaviour therapy effected no more change than treatment as usual (Dawe et al., 1993). Perhaps more importantly, research did show that the craving levels achieved in the "laboratory" did not bear any resemblance to the craving that patients experienced when they left the inpatient unit (Powell et al., 1993). It was folly to promise too much in the first place and the experiments showed that progress might be best achieved via the elimination of hypotheses and misconceptions.

The pleasure paradox of addiction

If behavioural attempts to tackle addiction fall short then the alternative might be to develop approaches that can interrogate the deeper motivations of using. Herein, it seems to me that the alternative to a model of diversion or aversion therapy is one that starts by considering the allure of the addiction in the first place. The will to pleasure in drug use is that which is compelling. But there appears to be a palpable tension inherent in misuse, whereby the peak experience of pleasure exists at a threshold of danger or risk. There appears to be a pleasure-pain dichotomy where the oppositional drives of life and death, connoted by Freud as Eros and Thanatos respectively, push and pull in different directions. I have listened to many conversations among groups of addicts, where the discussion has turned from sentimental reminiscences of old haunts and habits, to an almost obligatory contest as to who has been on the most dangerous binge, who has lost the most money, or who has endured the most horrific overdose, and so on. These life and death stories possess a kind of perverse exhibitionism, the bravado of courting danger.

When we consider these dangerous activities in the pursuit of sensual and psychic hedonism, we seem to be in the domain of human experience that is beyond the pleasure principle (Freud, 1920). That is to say, pleasure is not the endgame, rather it exists in relation to an urge to pain and even death. Death defying feats of ingestion, or the repetition of pain in self-puncturing with a needle; these are the moments where danger weaves with rapture. The prospect of a life-threatening disease or sudden death from overdosing on an adulterated intoxicant can seemingly be considered in the same orbit. It is the ecstatic feeling of intoxication that runs the user into the pathway of self-destructiveness and sometimes death. Giving up the urge to pleasure may be less challenging than alleviating the urge to danger and death. This is apparent in the habitual act of self-cutting. For some people, cutting becomes a way of alleviating tension and an array of feelings that are otherwise unwanted. Rage and anger in particular seem to feature in cases of cutting, where fury at another person can be controlled and honed into an act of self-cutting and bloodletting. Cutting can become highly compulsive, and clients can find it difficult to give it up, much in the same way that a drug addict finds it difficult to give up their drug of choice.

The worst consequences of the pleasure paradox are all too apparent. Spike was a heroin user in his late forties. He had been nicknamed by those who knew him because he had been injecting for so long. He had become the collapse between his signifier (his name) and his signified (his preoccupation with intravenous drugs). Spike was a symbolic equation; the needle was no longer external to him, rather he was the thing itself. Spike was reminiscent of Cocteau's (1930) sketches in *Opium* where the craving for opium was so strong that figures were morphed into a plethora of opium pipes, with orifices and limbs resembling pipes. It was as if Cocteau could not see beyond his craving, and that such was the intensity of appetite for opium that he imagined himself as a body of pipes ready to smoke. In the same way, Spike's body seemed to be the consequence of craving, except for Spike it was not pipes but injecting wounds and infections that covered his body.

I worked with Spike for several months as an outpatient until he eventually gave in and gathered himself to come in for an admission to the inpatient unit. On the day of his admission I met him at the hospital reception. The inpatient unit was a five minute walk from the reception through the lovely grounds of the Bethlem Hospital. On the way back Spike was limping badly, and said he'd had pain in his leg for some days. Upon examination his leg was swollen like a balloon and the injecting site in his groin, one of the few remaining accessible veins, was badly infected, the size of a tennis ball and seeping puss like a mini volcano. An ambulance was called and Spike was taken off to Accident & Emergency forthwith, and a deep vein thrombosis was confirmed a few hours later. On return to the hospital, Spike seemed ebullient. He told us: "The doctor said that *one more* injection might have killed me."

To describe Spike's condition in terms of "self-harm" rather belies the social impact of his condition. Within hours of an initial contact with Spike, I worked out that the ripple effect of his condition had touched the lives of some twenty or so health staff: the hospital porter who had helped Spike limp to the unit, the two nurses who assessed him on arrival, the ambulance controller, the two ambulance staff, the Accident & Emergency receptionist, and other attending doctors and nurses that saw him. That was before he was admitted to a ward where another array of staff would have seen Spike. And all of this without taking into account the other patients and staff on the inpatient drug unit who had met Spike and seen him whisked off in no time, left with anxiety about his crisis. Over a period of one week from admission, Spike's affliction was vicariously, and not so subtly, inflicted on numerous others.

The notion of self-harm in this sense seems a poor explanation of the phenomena of the event. We might think of it rather as a sort of "butterfly-spike-effect", that is to say the more serious the act of self-harm, the greater the impact on others (a statistical "spike"). The butterfly-spike-effect conjures up an image of a sharp injection that at first appears to be surgically interior to the injector but in the consequences erupts into a toxic entanglement that seeps outwards, as in the butterfly effect of chaos theory, where a butterfly flaps its wings in the east, a wind blows in the west. In envisaging the weeping damage from a needlestick wound we can contemplate the potential for the risk of infection from damaged skin, either by *skin popping* (subcutaneous injecting) or intravenous injecting. Drug users may use the same ever blunting needles and syringe several times, failing to clean the site before injecting takes place. Complications arising from non-aseptic injecting practice include: abscesses, allergic reactions, endocarditis, osteomyelitis, septicaemia, thrombophlebitis, and gangrene. These are often considered as private hazards, but more crucially, such self-damage is implicit to the risk of cross-infection through the process of sharing drugs and injecting equipment.

Death in Spike's case oozed from his very psychic and physical pores. The idea of a pleasurable ingestion of a drug in his case, like many others, collapses into an array of pain and hurt. We might say that there is *no such thing as an act of self-harm*. Instead, the harm always has consequences and impact on others. The idea of self-in-constant flow with others is not new of course. Winnicott tells us there is no such thing as baby; show me a baby, he says, and there will be a mother. There is empirical evidence that the self-harm of the drug user is not an isolated event, rather it is derived from a long-standing self-other system of harm. In a detailed doctoral study, Christine English (2011) has drawn attention to the fact that among her study cohort of thirty drug addicts, all the subjects had experienced some considerable level of violence and cruelty during childhood. English's findings indicate that, at least among her study cohort, drug use in adulthood is a recycling of prior experiences of hurt and harm in childhood.

Negotiating the terrain of pleasure through infancy to adulthood is a problem for most of us at some time or other in our lives. Many people develop occasional excessive appetites if not more elongated dependencies, to substances that have mind-altering potential such as tea, caffeine, cigarettes, alcohol, and chocolate. Taken to excess, indulgence in these pleasures of ingestion can have serious long-term consequences which may be life-threatening. Other people become "hooked" on different indulgences that may not cause immediate or long-term physical danger but can produce serious emotional difficulties. For instance, the pleasurable pursuit of gambling can become an all-consuming destructive pastime. Gamblers Anonymous offers a successful support network following the same model of support as Alcoholics Anonymous (AA) and Narcotics Anonymous (NA). Other recreational pursuits such as fast cars, rock climbing, parachute jumping and more lately bungee jumping are notable as all having a high degree of social acceptance and a high degree of risk.

Some of these extreme activities stimulate the production of endorphins, the body's own natural opiates, and participants often refer to becoming addicted to experiencing the "buzz" of participation in extreme sports. *The Face* magazine in March 1997 had an article called "Climbing versus Clubbing" in which they invited a group of drug-taking club-goers and a group of climbers to swap activities for a weekend. The "chemical kick" of getting high in a club was compared to the adrenaline kick of literally getting geographically high, suggesting cognate psychobiological processes. However, one of the climbers said that the buzz from scaling a mountain was preferable to the chemical high because the climbing high could last for months whereas the high from taking a drug only felt "good for eight hours and then shitty for forty".

The relationship between legal acts of extreme pleasure-seeking and more dangerous compulsions sit along a "pleasure abuse continuum". At one end there are the more innocuous compulsions where harm is less or slower over a longer period, and at the other extreme there is addiction to powerfully volatile substances and mind-altering experiences that carry a greater immediate threat of dangerousness. In-between these poles there are a range of drug and non-drug pursuits, no less pathological, which might be considered with varying degrees of risk. The willing flirtation with dangerousness and self-destruction characterizes the drift from one end of the spectrum to the other. It is the nature of this envelopment in death at the far reach of the spectrum that is worth unpicking in order to extrapolate back to the other less immediate, though no less worrying, addictions such as smoking.

Freud's "nirvana principle" and dependency on death

Death is so indubitably bound up with drug addiction that it is idiosyncratically a fact of life for many users. My aim in this next section is to try to unfold the phenomenon of death's allure in drug addiction, tracing back concepts derived from Freud's (1920) model of the death instinct through to Fairbairn's (1930) idea of a "death impulse". Even though there are divergences in these models they each converge in practice where there can be no avoiding the clinical reality of the dangerous drug user seemingly keeping death as a close companion.

Drug use offers an ideal mechanism for "splitting off" bad and negative feelings. That is to say, chemical intoxication brings about euphoric states that can hold unwanted feelings states at bay. In *Go Ask Alice*, the diary based on the real chronicles of a teenage drug user, we can see from one day to the next how the pharmaceutical intoxication creating a sense of "being on top of the world" can supersede the feelings of hopelessness and distress caused by the upheaval that the diarist is facing in moving house, changing schools, and so on, at a critical time in her adolescent life. The process of splitting off the bad feelings is an attempt to nullify all feelings and thoughts through the creation of a chemically induced pleasurable state of mind. This "retreat" from reality might be compared to a schizoid type mental state where the chemical state of mind becomes a defence against reality (Steiner, 1993). Intoxication as a state of unthinkingness, as a psychotic retreat from the social world, was something which appealed to both Rosenfeld and Bion in their work in the 1960s when they started to see drug users alongside their case loads of schizophrenics (which I discuss in more detail in chapter Six).

But one of the features of the psychotic retreat that we seem to overlook is the lurch towards death. More than any other psychiatric patient group, drug users exemplify Henri Rey's (1994) observation that clinical presentations are littered with images and identifications with death. Rey was describing the fact that so many of his clients seemed to bring dreams of graveyards, or dreams of people dying, to talk about in therapy. Part of the challenge in therapy is to help the addict de-identify from the allure of death. For example, Elaine was 41 years old when she was admitted for detoxification and rehabilitation. She had a twenty-year history of substance abuse and was admitted for inpatient treatment a few months after the deaths of her husband, who had died of a drug overdose, and her father, both within a few days of each other. She was isolated from her own family and the family of her husband too and, without any consideration to her feelings, both funerals were arranged on the same day. In the end Elaine went to the funeral of her husband.

Her admission for inpatient treatment coincided with the first anniversary of both deaths. As she withdrew from heroin the mental pain associated with the losses resurfaced with great force. Her use of opiates had numbed not only her body but also her mind. Whereas she had been preoccupied with ingesting drugs, without the cushion of opiates she now found herself ruminating about dying in order to be reunited with her husband. She spoke about her and her husband's habit of frequenting graveyards when they were taking drugs; she said they had been "happy among the dead" and that they used to listen to "songs from the grave". And now she longed to be with her husband again. She seemed to literally "love him to death". She became suicidal and needed around the clock care and observation, which was delivered by staff and fellow residents (an innovation for the hospital at the time, and something which was ethically thorny, but very successful). As Elaine's feelings subsided she asked if she could visit the graves of both her husband and father and this was organized; and with the support of her key worker, Sarah Robson, Elaine took flowers to the graves and read words she had chosen beforehand. Over subsequent weeks the intensity of her suicidal feelings abated.

Elaine's over-identification with her dead husband and father was a fractured point in mourning which was manifest in a malady of self-homicidal urges. It was through a new synthesis of mourning, some guided by the staff, that she was able to begin the process of facing up to the losses and then working through them to the point of de-identification. The original mourning had been thwarted by the use of drugs at the time of the funerals and the period after. The sober revisiting of the graves during treatment seemed to act as a new location point from mourning and recovery. The mourning ritual needed to be repeated following detoxification when the impact of the loss could be more realistically emotionally encountered. In Elaine's case it seemed that the source of death's identification had been located and there was then a possibility that her unconscious urge towards self-homicide could be quelled. This was the beginning for a review of other losses in her life, the first stage of a rigorous inventory going back beyond the years of her drug use to the losses that appeared to be the prequel to addiction.

Rey (1994) argues that these types of dead objects are continually resurrected in imaginings and dreams in order that they can be subject to reparation. This repetitive act of living-death resurrection, as I described earlier, can be denoted as a specific object-relations syndrome deriving from the myth of Prometheus. A more general supposition about the phenomenon of identification with death might lead us to consider the way a drug invokes a sort of death-sleep. In addiction treatments, death appears like a tangible object: dream images in individual and group psychotherapy, headstones, crosses, skulls, and so on represented in creative therapies, music that celebrates death, tattoos that depict death—in the next chapter we will hear about Lucy's skull tattoo called the Holey Ghost (sic)—and so on. Many patients carry jarring images of the corpses of fellow addicts and memories of overdoses. The spectre of fatal diseases such as HIV and hepatitis hover over addiction and impress further the threshold of life and death that characterizes chronic drug use. The milieu of an addictions unit is so infused with death sometimes that it often seems like an object floating in the very spaces between people. Elaine's case above suggests that the urge towards death needs to be faced, understood, and worked through.

Working in the shadow of death

The identification with death may also be resonant for staff who are drawn to work in the field. It always seems a noteworthy career choice to elect to work with drug users, especially as it stands out in terms of the number of young casualties that one is likely to encounter. Alison was in her early twenties when she started working on an inpatient drug dependency treatment unit. Not long after she had begun on the unit one of the staff team died unexpectedly. And then a few weeks later one of the inpatients died on the ward. While most of Alison's workmates attended the funeral of the colleague and then later the memorial service for the patient, Alison did not go to either, saying she wanted to deal with her grief in her own way. Over the next few months Alison increasingly struggled with her work. On night duty one time, Alison reported that she had felt so ill at ease that she had run past the room where the patient had died. In supervision she described feeling "bad vibes, chills, and superstitions". It was a bad time on the ward: one of the patients had reported seeing a ghost and there were whisperings about the room where the patient had died as being somehow jinxed. There was a general uncanny atmosphere hanging over the community, and Alison seemed most susceptible. In clinical supervision Alison explored her urge to run away from what she called the "haunted room". She said she had become aware that the recent deaths had reawakened her feelings about the death of her best friend who, at the age of nine had been knocked down and killed on the way to school. Alison said that she had not been allowed to go to the funeral. As Alison's supervisor,

I felt obliged to point out the parallel: as she had not been allowed to go to the funeral of her friend, she had not allowed herself to attend the funeral and memorial service of the colleague and the patient. She became furious with me and said it was "all sick, sick" and stormed out of the session.

A few months later, after a week's annual leave, Alison returned to work. In supervision she told me that she had visited the grave of her best friend while she was on holiday. She explained how there was a picture of her best friend (aged nine) waxed onto the headstone. Alison described the experience of visiting the grave had "brought things flooding back". We talked further about her friend. She said she had often imagined what would her friend be like, what job she would be doing, what height she would be, and so on. Alison seemed to have kept her friend growing up with her. I said it seemed that rather than bear the loss of the young friend it was as if she had kept her alive like a ghost. It was as if Alison had not been able to bury her friend. But the return to the grave, and the image of the friend waxed onto the headstone had jolted a new process of mourning. Over subsequent months Alison reported feeling relief from the previous anxieties she had felt at work. Not long afterwards Alison left the unit and went on to another field of mental health work. It was as if the repeating death of the friend could be laid to rest, and she could at last move on.

I think Alison's experience illuminates for us a ubiquitous dynamic that begs the question: how do we understand the nature of this type of compulsive or repeating identification with death? Freud's (1920) thesis in *Beyond the Pleasure Principle* was that the pursuit of finding pleasure in life was confounded by an innate tendency to repeat masochistic acts, that the will to pleasure was countered by a drive towards destruction. He made the bold and controversial assertion that this dual drive operated at the cusp of a biological imperative that influenced the mind and the action of the organism, and he described it as an instinctual drive which he called "the death instinct". Evidence for the death instinct, said Freud, had its basis in the molecular investigations of biologists at the time who had found that the life cycle of cells innately compelled them to return to inorganic status. Freud hypothesized that this cellular activity had a manifest impact on the total organism, leading to a psychic desire for quietude and removal of all tension to point zero, inertia, an overlay of experience at the meeting point of sleep and death. This was an apt poetical designation on Freud's part that evoked the last reckoning of the romantic poets, like Keats and Shelley, who vividly described sleep and death conjoined in joyous union. In order to convey the strange euphoric dualism of life and death, Freud adopted the term "nirvana principle".

The idea of the nirvana principle was quickly developed by Barbara Low (1920), one of the founder members of the London Institute of Psychoanalysis, who published one of the first introductory books on psychoanalysis. Low (1920) used the idea of nirvana to depict the ordinary desire to return to an omnipotent state of bliss in infancy. But in adopting the term himself, Freud reloaded the concept with an altogether darker hue, alluding to the tension in Buddhist philosophy where the idea of nirvana can mean both a perfected meditative state of harmonious contemplation of the self with nature, but also complete annihilation. The term was apposite and true to the complexities of the organism's instinctive wish to reach a point of extinction, a final return to the inorganic (Freud, 1920, p. 50). If Freud had at first oscillated as to whether this principle might be more inclined towards the life-preserving forces of Eros, a few years later in his paper "The Economic Problem of Masochism" (1924) he finally posited the nirvana principle in the service of the death instinct. It is of note that Freud began the paper by suggesting that perplexities of masochism were such that they seemed instinctually to overhaul the ordinary search for pleasure in a manner which he compared to the effects of a drug:

> The existence of a masochistic trend in the instinctual life of human beings may justly be described as mysterious from the economic point of view. For if mental processes are governed by the pleasure principle in such a way that their first aim is the avoidance of unpleasure and the obtaining of pleasure, masochism is incomprehensible. If pain and unpleasure can not be simply warnings but actually aims, the pleasure is paralysed—it is as though the watchmen over our mental life were put out of action by a drug (Freud, 1924, p. 155).

It was the fact that even the most considered psychoanalytic endeavours were not reaching some of his patients who, quite beyond reason, continued their steady spiral of repetitious self-harm in spite of Freud's best efforts. Freud was drawn to postulate that there was a force of death, a primal masochism, patrolling the reservoir of the id. Freud surmised that his new theory might be "incomprehensible" to his students but he nonetheless "pushed forward ever unsubdued" (1920, fn. p. 36). It was ultimately a depressing diagnosis in that he finally saw that mankind was destined to grapple with the instinct for death because as far as he could see there was no such thing as an instinct for perfection. Of course, the context of Freud's bleak prognosis needs to be located against the dark backdrop of the First World War where his anxieties about his two soldier sons were ever present. And perhaps more importantly, the theory of the death instinct emerged in the aftermath of the death of his beloved and precious daughter Sophie. But the context of the theory in this sense, albeit of terrible loss, does not undermine its voracity, rather we might say Freud grasps close the truth of human nature at an exceedingly dark hour.

Freud encountered death agitating his theories and all previous axioms were thrown into question in light of new thoughts on death. The theoretical path of the death instinct was uneasy, even for many of his most faithful followers. Though the idea for some was seen to be of useful clinical utility in adducing the biological and psychological exchange of organic entropy (Bernfeld & Feitlberg, 1931), for Fairbairn (1930) it did not sit so comfortably. Fairbairn offered a studious critical rebuttal of the death instinct theory, arguing that the instinct of animals in the wild was not so much driven by a death instinct to kill, rather the process of killing was for food and therefore death was an incidental consequence of a self-preservation drive for life. Fairbairn felt that the being of man was likewise driven by the need for sustenance and that all instincts were essentially expressions of life (1930, p. 122). Sadism was therefore not driven by a death instinct and nor was death the object of a sadistic aim (1930, p. 123). In considering the concept of cellular death, from which Freud began, Fairbairn preferred to follow Freud's own observation that tissue culture experiments had demonstrated that in favourable circumstances, a community of cells would assure tissue multiplication *ad infinitum*. Fairbairn argued that Freud was too much in the grip of his own theory of "auto-eroticism"—an account of the individual as inwardly folded with the pleasures of the world as self-derivative—to embrace any alternative notion that might be more object related.

Fairbairn felt that the death drive in essence was more like an impulse directed towards an external environment and that this impulse towards death was the result of experience rather than an innate drive.

He concluded that Freud's theory was fundamentally flawed because it was "derived not from psychology but biology" (1930, p. 127). Thus, Fairbairn postulated his own praxis: "Would it not be more natural to regard death impulses as instances of the instinct of aggression being deflected inwards from external objects to the ego than to regard aggressive impulses as instances of death instincts being deflected outwards from the ego to external objects?" (1930, p. 127).

Klein (1946) began by accepting Freud's given of the existence of the death instinct, arguing that the infant's death instinct was the source of inner anxiety that could be projected and become attached to external objects. The infant then believed that external objects would retaliate and thus the infant phantasized that it would be annihilated. Ostensibly, the maelstrom of primitive trauma Klein saw as populating the external world of objects around the infant were derived from the death instinct. She noted that the earliest objects were experienced as parts of the whole, such as the breast, the nipple, or the penis, which became the feared objects of death, if initially only through their absence. It was within this exchange between the mind of the infant and the sense of death in the outside world, that was formed the crux in which healthy maturation and growth needed to take place. Insofar as the mother internalized the unthinkable anxiety about death in the infant's instinctive mind, the mother offered a sense of protection and triumph of the life instinct. That is to say, as the infant externalized its fear and anxiety the mother contained the anxiety before returning it in a diluted and less frightening form. Thus the mother reassured the infant that the world was not going to end.

In Klein's model, the death instinct existed from the beginning and was therefore adumbrated by a process of parental containment. She followed Freud's idea that Eros triumphed over Thanatos but in describing the death instinct in terms of a fluid interchange between internal and external states, she arbitrated a bridge between Freud (too preoccupied with auto-eroticism) and Fairbairn who was mostly concerned with the externality of object relations.

Addicted to near life: shifting dependencies, from pleasure to persons

It is not uncommon when the addict seeks professional help in the first place that they deny that they need "people" to help them; they say all they are looking for is a prescription, and an endless supply of their drug. The need or desire for interpersonal affiliation is denied. I have worked with many addicts as outpatients in preparation for inpatient treatment and the most common complaint is that they do not want to have to talk to anyone. Methadone maintenance programmes have been a key hinge in drug treatment services, debatably serving a function in enticing clients into treatment. We might say that the desire for a script somatically represents the exchange between the therapist and the addict. It may take months or years before the identified need for the drug is converted from its biological and chemical basis to its psychological substrate. From the perspective of examining the symbolism of the triangular relationship between the therapist, the addicted patient, and the drug, there are a some helpful reference points that offer a psychodynamic prolegomenon that would be useful reading for any student or practitioner (Abraham, 1927; Glover, 1932; Fenichel, 1945; Rosenfeld, 1960; Kohut, 1971; Wurmser, 1974; Limentani, 1986; Kaufman, 1991; Rosenfeld, 1992; Van Schoor, 1992; Hopper, 1995).

The shift from this chemical dependency to human dependency is characterized by increasing reliance either on a therapist or on a group of fellow patients in recovery. This is the case during the process of residential treatment in a therapeutic community, or in Narcotics Anonymous where the group becomes the key point of attachment. I will try to illustrate this process of shifting dependency with reference to a clinical case. Ahmed was a heroin addict in his early thirties. He was a reserved man whose manner tended to give the impression that he felt himself to be somehow superior. He had been treated in private clinics but with little success. On admission to an NHS inpatient unit he said he was not convinced that his residential treatment was a good use of his hard-pressed time. His withdrawal from heroin was probably no more difficult than usual, with a range of physical and psychological withdrawal symptoms: cramps, sleep deprivation, anxiety, sickness, appetite loss, and so on. It was, however, searing headaches that bothered Ahmed the most. Attempts to control the headaches using hot baths, tiger balm, massage and herbal teas, as well as support in therapy sessions, all proved unsuccessful in alleviating them. After five days of his ten-day methadone withdrawal Ahmed was on the verge of leaving the unit. As a last resort Ahmed was prescribed paracetamol. It was a rare event for paracetamol to be prescribed on the unit so it was subject to much discussion in the therapy groups for some days afterwards.

Ahmed took paracetamol on two separate occasions. His headaches lessened in intensity and he stayed to complete his withdrawal, and he embarked on a programme of intensive therapy and rehabilitation of up to six weeks.

After several weeks he had begun to settle well into the treatment programme. He progressed on to the pass system which enabled him to gradually increase the time he spent away from the unit on his own, starting with a few hours before moving on to longer passes week by week up to a day pass and finally weekend leave. On return from his first day pass Ahmed reported that he had been craving more than he had anticipated and admitted that having returned to "an old haunt" he had come close to using. His specimen result later confirmed that he had not used. He said he had refrained from using because at the point when he had been tempted he had been surprised by an image that had come quite unexpectedly into his mind. The image was this: he said he saw his key therapist "running down the corridor of the ward with two paracetamol in a beaker". Ahmed said that this image in his mind had given him the resolve not to use because he did not want to let his key worker down.

The image summoned up in Ahmed's mind may represent something of how a process of internalizing a human relationship can come to replace the allure of chemicals. Ahmed's key worker had indeed dispensed paracetamol to him, although she had certainly not "run down the corridor". We might say that the ordinary professional concern of the key worker, who was very experienced, had become a rather idealized item in Ahmed's mind; she had of course been mindful of Ahmed's urge to leave the unit prematurely but had taken this as usual in her stride. In Ahmed's mind he had turned this into a running delivery of his painkillers. Nonetheless, this imago of concern appeared strong enough to prevent him from using drugs, at least on this occasion. We might say that the key worker had come to represent something of a transitional person or object that mediated between Ahmed's drug hunger and his desire for what would appear to be a doting carer in his time of need. That is to say, in Ahmed's mind, there was *an inter-relationship between the objects of the beaker, the drugs, and the key therapist.* In the first place the objects were the hard pills which we might think of in terms of being autistic type objects (Rosenfeld, 1992), characterized by cold and inhuman sensual states, which were connected in his mind to the caring urgency of the key worker. The image was suggestive of the bargaining that was going on in Ahmed's mind between his addicted self that believed that he could only be in a reliable relationship with a chemical and a new synthesis of self connected and receptive to human exchange. Having "split off" and denied the real significance of the care and support that he might receive from someone else (beginning with the staff and his key worker), his therapy was a process of discovering that relationships might be potentially life sustaining.

The way in which clients shift their attachment or dependency from drugs onto their therapist and peers during treatment might even be described as a default process in a good outcome in therapy. This default dynamic is not just limited to working with addicts, rather it is the basis of many interpersonal procedures of talking treatments in counselling, psychotherapy, and psychoanalysis. Balint (1968) described how a therapeutic relationship has the potential to engender an addiction-like dependency in the patient. We might say that in relation to patients who are trying to give up their compulsive behaviours, the intensity of their attachment to their obsessions is switched to their intensity of attachment to their therapist. In the first place the therapist is often perceived as an omnipotent and gratifying object, but then like a drug object that is craved the therapist is seen as depriving in their absence. The therapist needs to contemplate how to manage the initial establishment of the therapeutic alliance, which is paramount in laying the foundations for ongoing work, in regard to the intense attachment and dependency that may emerge. In light of the need for informed consent to treatment, the therapist should outline for the new patient the likelihood of an intense attachment occurring. In my experience I have yet to see a patient successfully complete a detoxification and an initial period of recovery without the emergence of an intense attachment. The attachment may emerge between a pair of patients, and while this is not always problematic, it has always seemed preferable that the attachment is directed towards a group of patients or a member of staff.

Building a rapport offers the patient a safe place to begin, a place to discuss feelings which have remained repressed, often for many years. This rapport, when set within consistent frames of time and place becomes a "potential space" within which the therapy may unfold (Winnicott, 1971). Thus, if a patient is frightened about physical withdrawal or craving drugs, but not yet able to put these fears into words, then the nonverbal or unconscious network of communication is imperative and the therapist needs to have some understanding of these unconscious forms of communication. The therapist uses their own reaction to the patient as a tool for understanding how the patient might be feeling. The patient's primary projective processes, the externalization of feeling states that are not always modified by mature articulation, are considered as healthy and adaptive forms of communication in the early stages of treatment where the patient can not find the words to communicate how they are feeling (Sandler, 1988). The patient may also use concrete issues to convey their distress where psychic complaint can become somatized, as in Ahmed's case. Thus, early interventions during the withdrawal phase of treatment see the staff in a holding role which often has the air of a maternal engagement, making sure the patient eats and hydrates, even when their appetite is poor, offering comfort and reassurance and so forth when anxiety becomes unbearable. Dynamic or analytical approaches are often criticized for drawing attention to the interpersonal dependency needs of the patient but I think this criticism is misplaced because it is by recognizing and managing dependency needs that they can be worked through.

While it cannot be entirely dismissed that some therapists may indeed be seduced by the dependency of the patient, most psychodynamic counselling and psychotherapy trainings in the UK require therapists to be in therapy themselves as part of the training. One hopes that the narcissistic urges of the therapist, a need to be needed so to speak, have been addressed in personal therapy. It should be added that even in therapeutic approaches where the issue of the patient's relationship to the therapist is not focused on, this does not preclude that these therapists might have a pathological wish for their patient to be dependent on them. Indeed, a period of personal therapy and ongoing clinical supervision would be indicated for all professionals including nurses, psychiatrists, social workers, psychologists, and others, where there is an opportunity to have a training experience of tackling and understanding their own dependency needs. In my experience where there has been this experience there is less likelihood that these therapists will engender a pathological dependency among their patients.

The therapist's *acceptance* of the patient's need for a new experience of benign dependency is imperative if the patient is to replace their prior notion of malignant dependency which will have formed across many years, finally becoming embedded in the rituals of chemical dependency. The *fear* of interpersonal dependency is therefore encased in the patient's response to treatment, but it is also a preponderant anxiety that undermines many psychiatric treatments. This anxiety emerged during the 1980s when there was a determined effort by government to dilute what was felt to be a "nanny" approach to welfare in the UK. Patients were encouraged to spend less time in hospital and become more inclined towards self-care and less reliant or dependent on professional. While some of this philosophy in psychiatric services may have been attuned towards a progressive agenda of deconstructing the unnecessary of ills of institutionalization for some psychiatric patients, the government agenda was largely determined by economic forces rather than coherent service configuration (Barham, 1992). Pedder (2010) has argued that the attempt to eradicate patient dependency was misguided, arguing it arose from a much wider Western cultural proclivity towards individualism. Pedder further suggested that the model of mature dependency in Eastern cultures like Japan might offer much that the West might learn from.

It is tricky to negotiate through the philosophic intricacies of dependency. But we might say that the starting point of recovery from addictions, compulsions, and other mental disorders for that matter, is not one of fostering dependency but rather one of *allowing* it to emerge as a treatment concomitant. This becomes a different model to the outmoded idea of "regression therapy" which was practised more widely in the 1960s and 1970s (though some remnants of the approach still exist in some schools of psychotherapy), where the patient was encouraged to return to earlier developmental stages where trauma might have first occurred. The idea of allowing issues of dependency to occur of their own volition is a very different frame within which to approach the concept of dependency. The dynamics of shifting malign dependencies and the emergence of a new synthesis of benign dependency exists in the fulcrum of the interpersonal relationship between the therapist and the patient. It has been suggested that there is a valid role of the "therapist as friend" in addiction programmes that can be cast in terms of a modified aspect of "transference" (Strang, 1982).

However, while a "positive transference" (Freud, 1912) may be the basis of establishing a milieu conducive to treatment, I have mostly found it is in the working through of the negative transference where the most therapeutic purchase can be located. It is where the therapist is seen *more like a fiend than a friend* where the gains are truly made. We might say that the preferred positive transference is that which has been earned through overcoming the negative transference, so to speak. The negative transference does not have to be forced to exist; it is enough that the therapist is alert and attuned to the possibility of the patient's negative emotional states and these will, sure enough, be forthcoming. Most substance misusers struggle to deal with negative emotional states, feelings of sadness, loss, and separation and these feeling have been shown to be those which are most likely to be the cause of a relapse following sobriety (Marlatt & Gordon, 1985). The process of therapy therefore involves a rehabilitation in the experience of being with these negative emotional states without the nullifying prop of chemical support. Events that involve facing sadness and loss are opportunities for therapeutic encounters: real life in small doses, so to speak. It is inevitable that during the course of treatment these negative emotional states, communicated somatically in the first place perhaps, as was the case with Ahmed, are eventually raised to the level of interpersonal exploratory therapy. Bad and unwanted aspects of the self may be contained either by the individual therapist or the group (or both in treatment centres that offer a combined treatment approach of group and individual therapy) before being re-integrated by a patient in a way that exerts less disturbance.

CHAPTER SIX

Major Tom, Lucy, Bion, and the psychotic vacuum[1]

Oddity

This chapter brings together three separate case studies which form an illustrative tripod drawing attention to a particular feature of repetition-compulsion which I refer to as the "psychotic vacuum". I begin with a case anecdote about an amphetamine user who was much taken with David Bowie's song *Space Oddity* which he said spoke to him about his experience of tripping. He had suffered from amphetamine psychosis, though even when drug free after several weeks in residential treatment he still displayed features of what appeared to be an underlying psychotic condition. His sense of being adrift, like Major Tom in Bowie's song looking down on the earth from outside himself, seemed to seemed to encapsulate the essence of how he got on with other people in general, as if he was indeed in a relational vacuum. In the chapter I also look at Bion's theory where he makes a link between drug addiction and schizophrenia. In particular I reflect on a small piece of archival research I undertook in Bion's library where I found a copy of Rosenfeld's (1965)

---

[1]A version of this paper was presented at the Annual Community Housing and Therapy (CHT) Trust *Addiction & Psychosis* Conference held at the Royal Society of Medicine, March 5, 2010.

book *Psychotic States*. Bion had made copious notes in the margins of one chapter where Rosenfeld presented his central exposition about drug addiction. Some of Bion's marginal notes begin to coalesce in a new idea of psychotic fixation and repetition-compulsion. Drawing on one of Bion's own case accounts and his observation of a client with a particular ritual whereby, upon lowering himself onto the couch, the patient would appear to evacuate Bion into a corner of the room, I develop a theory of a "psychotic vacuum". In the last case presentation, I look at the life and death of one of my former clients, Lucy Cameron. I look in particular at her poem *The Space*, which was published posthumously. Lucy's poem helps us towards an understanding of the devastating psychotic space that is all too apparent in the ravaged lives of many people whose relationships are severed by substance misuse.

Countdown

Part of the momentum for this chapter was a piece of unexpected good fortune in the course of doing some research into Bion's work with the playwright Samuel Beckett. Francesca Bion (Bion's widow) kindly permitted me the opportunity to spend the day interviewing her about Beckett and Bion among other things, and then she allowed me some time in Bion's library. I was interested to see if any of Beckett's books were in Bion's collection, to see if there was any evidence that Bion had been interested in the trajectory of his former client. Actually, I found little to go on there were a few of Beckett's plays (*Waiting for Godot*, *Endgame*), and biographies of Beckett by James Knowlson and Deidre Bair, but no annotations or inserted notes. But it was during the course of my browsing that I happened across a copy of Herbert Rosenfeld's (1965) *Psychotic States*. There is probably much more to be said about Bion's and Rosenfeld's personal relationship, but I had previously known that both Rosenfeld and Bion were working with drug users in the early 1960s. Rosenfeld's *Psychotic States* is a sustained effort to interrogate drug addiction with a particular emphasis on psychosis. This idea was given a similar overhaul by Bion a few years later in *Second Thoughts* (1967), where he tells us that he took his work with two drug addicts and four patients with schizophrenia as his point of departure. And so it was with some prior interest that I opened up Bion's copy of Rosenfeld's book. Apart from noting that Bion obviously had no qualms about makes his own notes on the pages of a printed book, it was the sheer copiousness of his margin writings that was breathtaking. Indeed in one chapter, which I talk about in more detail later, Bion appears to have been moved to fill almost every available margin space with his own critique.

The diagnostic challenge of differentiating between drug-induced psychosis and psychosis *per se* is not straightforward, and to some extent we can say that this conundrum preoccupied both Bion and Rosenfeld in the early 1960s. The question for them was; what can we tell about the mind of the compulsive drug user when we compare it with the mind of the person suffering from psychosis? There tends to be a chicken and the egg debate about which comes first, the substance misuse or the psychosis? More lately, the term "dual diagnosis" has been adopted to describe the interweave of more than one presenting mental health issue, that is to say, there can be two conditions that can contribute to a mental health problem. For instance, is it possible to have a drug problem and a concurrent depression? Of course the answer is yes, but for many practitioners in the field of substance misuse the concern about drugs outweighs the concern about the underlying depression. But I have always subscribed to the notion that drug addiction is a symptom of an underlying mental health problem, and not the problem itself. Dual diagnosis has been a helpful psychiatric categorization because it appeals to the idea that drug problems are not unilinear but rather converging from an array of other mental health vulnerabilities.

At the risk of short-circuiting a debate about what we might mean by psychosis and schizophrenia, it is worth mentioning briefly some of the theories that might be anchors for us. When it comes to the social construction of psychosis, its political and familial antecedents, there is no doubt that R. D. Laing's contribution is scintillating. Laing and his colleagues saw schizophrenia as a process whereby one person might contain the madness on behalf of a family; the work thereafter was to be focused on a composite system rather than on the so-called identified patient. Having begun with Laing, through a route charted in the main by Klein and Bion, I worked with Murray Jackson at the Maudsley for several years and was introduced by Murray to Henri Rey. Rey (1994) delved into an array of borderline states, including psychotic anorexia, pointing to the universal psychodynamics that underpin psychotic states, the confusion of objects and the challenge that faces the therapist in untangling the objects that have become, as Rey called it "doubly identified", that is to say, one object getting mixed up with another. There are excellent summaries of Rey's contribution by John Steiner (1995) and Murray Jackson (2002).

Jackson's (1994, 2001) own influence has been abiding. He is perhaps best known for *Unimaginable Storms* (1994) with Paul Williams, which is an account of a psychoanalytic approach to acute inpatient care. *Unimaginable Storms* features several interviews with psychotic patients conducted by Jackson, and the transcripts of the interviews lend us insight into the process of talking therapy applied to work with people suffering from psychosis. Rey's (1994) thoughts too on psycholinguistics, and how we might understand words as communication vessels, is indispensable to my mind when it comes to mapping out the challenge of psychotherapy with people suffering from psychosis. How to talk to people with psychosis has been a more recent project which has led colleagues to develop a manual of good humanistic practice for talking with acutely ill patients (Bowers et al., 2010). The simple principles of thoughtfulness, meaningful listening, and the effort to find words which can help stabilize the client are at the nub of talking therapies, and these ideas open up psychoanalytical principles that can be used by all mental health practitioners. Bob Hinshelwood (2001) likewise has been committed to transforming general psychiatry and its allied professions with a view to the co-operation of the whole system in making sense of psychosis, finding ways to understand and construct the milieu in order to create the optimal conditions for patient recovery. Richard Lucas's (1993, 2009) idea of the "psychotic wavelength" is as neat and simple as it sounds: the therapist's challenge is to tune in, phasing out as much interference as possible, and finding the closest wavelength to focus on the first voice of the client, listen to what is being said through the noise of psychotic confusion. Finally, Joe Berke (2001, 2009, 2010) has illuminated us greatly, with his considerable experience since his early days with R. D. Laing, through his work with people suffering from psychosis at the Arbours Therapeutic Community in North London. Berke has continued to vitalize the debate about the therapeutic aspects of regression (2010), and the necessity of searching for meaning in madness. He is best known for his book with Mary Barnes, *A Journey Through Madness*, which was an innovative text that set a course for user involvement in research and writing about psychosis, therapy, and recovery.

Ground control

What underpins and links all the above people I have mentioned is that the search for meaning in psychosis is centrifugal. It is the idea that mental illness is a response to environmental and life trajectory events that distinguishes depth approaches from pharmaceutical; psychosis is seen as a coded communication that needs to be understood psychologically, rather than as a biological disequilibrium that needs to medically reverted. I have been fortunate, since the age of seventeen years when I started working as a support worker on the inpatient drug unit at the Bethlem Royal Hospital that I have been taught by colleagues who have been interested in the psychological depths of what ails the human condition, rather than the neurological proclivities. In other words, the mind has been more primary than the brain; mind over matter is the strap line. At the time when I started on the Drug Dependency Unit at the Bethlem Hospital, Phillip Connell was the medical consultant. Connell had established his reputation in the late 1960s with a theory about "amphetamine psychosis" (1968), after he had noticed the similarities between schizophrenia and the drug-induced mental state of some amphetamine users. In the mid 1960s, problem amphetamine misuse became increasingly apparent and the challenge of treating patients with drug misuse *and* psychiatric problems led to the first dedicated NHS service in the UK at the Maudsley. By situating the treatment of amphetamine addiction in the field of psychiatry, a precedent was set for the future medicalization of the treatment of addiction, a contested positioning ever since.

Although medically inclined, Connell was disposed to exploring the psychological depths of the intoxicated mind. I can recall several of Connell's interviews with inpatients but there was one patient in particular whom I remember. He was in his early thirties, an amphetamine user who had been admitted for detoxification from barbiturates followed by a period of rehabilitation. He was rather withdrawn, often uncommunicative. I spent many hours playing the guitar with him. He often played David Bowie's song *Space Oddity* a tale about an astronaut whose mission in space goes wrong and ends with his spacecraft malfunctioning and then drifting off into deep space, with Major Tom's final words: "Tell my wife I love her very much." My client said the song spoke to him because when he took speed he would experience being out of his body looking down on himself, something like Major Tom looking down at the earth from space. Of course, in the song Bowie had rather deftly paralleled the idea of the exploration of external space with the drug-induced search of internal space. The song was first released in 1969 to coincide with the moon landing of Apollo 11. The territory of outer space and the chemical reach to inner space had been imprinted on the cultural psyche by a generation whose experimentations with mind-altering substances were widespread. Student gurus like Herbert Marcuse (1968) were extolling the virtues of the liberation of the polity through hallucinogens, and psychotherapists like R. D. Laing were experimenting with LSD in psychotherapy, sometimes both therapist and client taking the drug to discover the impact on empathy (Laing, 1994). The space race had seen the USA win to put the first man on the moon, and the aphorism about Neil Armstrong (the first man to walk on the moon) talking to the hippy seems apposite:

Armstrong: We've got rockets to take us up, and capsules to bring us down.
    Hippy: Yeah man, I know!

In Bowie's song, Major Tom is initially something of a celebrity: "The newspapers want to know whose shirts you wear", and then we find Major Tom rather idyllically: "Floating in a tin can, far above the world, planet earth is blue and there's nothing I can do". But the song takes a dramatic turn when a fault means Major Tom loses control of his capsule and he drifts off out of orbit, into deep space: "… ground control to Major Tom, your circuit's dead there's something wrong, can you hear me Major Tom? Can you hear me Major Tom, can you …?". In the end Bowie's song isn't so much about the dangers of space travel, rather a warning about the consequences of a bad trip.

My guitar-playing patient said he identified with this feeling of being cut adrift. Perhaps it was the fear of being too far out, never to return, that had finally prompted him into treatment. Apart from playing the guitar with him, I thought him to be otherwise blunt and prickly. He was withdrawn from his fellow inpatients, and he did not have much to say for himself, either in therapy groups or over dinner. However, when he was interviewed by Phillip Connell, something quite different emerged. Connell always seemed somewhat aloof; his slicked-back hair and thick-rimmed glasses gave him a sort of detached austere air. One might not have expected him to connect with young drug users. But I saw how quickly Connell could put patients at ease. With a few well-chosen questions Connell cut to my guitar-playing patient's experience of amphetamine psychosis. It was soon apparent that his innermost thoughts were a maze of secret places, intricate keys, Beelzebub, gatekeepers, and conspiracies. Unbeknown to me he was living in a world of complex persecutions and paranoia. There was a palpable sense of relief for the client, who was able to unburden his thoughts. Perhaps it was because in Connell he detected a man on familiar territory: after all, Connell had, for twenty years or so, been investigating amphetamine psychosis. Though not a psychoanalyst, Connell seemed entirely at ease exploring the patient's delusions and hallucinations, and wondering about these in the same way that a psychoanalyst might approach a client's dream. It was a valuable lesson. After the interview with Connell, I was able to look afresh at my Major Tom patient, all those conspiracies and people out to get him; no wonder he kept himself to himself.

Stepping through the doors, floating in a most peculiar way

Connell was not alone, and nor was he the first, to consider an explanation for psychotic collapse in cases of substance misuse. In the late 1950s early 1960s psychoanalysts Herbert Rosenfeld and Wilfred Bion had been investigating the psychotic aspects of drug misuse. Bion and Rosenfeld were the favoured mentees of Melanie Klein, the relationship between Bion and Rosenfeld is of interest theoretically, but also personally. James Grotstein refers to an occasion, whereupon finishing a lecture, the first thing Bion was interested to know was: "What did Rosenfeld think?". There must have been some element of rivalry between Bion and Rosenfeld, perhaps even creative rivalry where they pushed forward ideas in reaction each other.

It was of some interest then that I happened across a copy of Rosenfeld's (1965) book *Psychotic States* in Bion's personal library. I was in Bion's library courtesy of Bion's widow as part of my research into Bion's analysis of Samuel Beckett. It was coincidental then that I took down Rosenfeld's book from the shelf to have a brief look. When I turned to Rosenfeld's chapter on drug addiction I was taken aback by the copious notes in the margin. I calculated that Bion's notes must have amounted to some 2,000 or so words altogether. Barely an inch was spared on any page. Bion's minute handwriting covered all available space. All the notes were made in black pen apart from one opening annotation which was made in blue (I wondered if this was a final summary produced later after further reflection, having read the whole chapter). As far as I could see from other books, though there were some marginal notes, the attention to detail and scale of the marginal notes in Rosenfeld's book was unusual. It seems that Rosenfeld was singled out for special attention.

More than half of Bion's comments on Rosenfeld's chapter mounted some disagreement or debate. In the text itself Bion had underlined sentences, for instance Rosenfeld's key assertion.

> My own psychoanalytic investigation of drug addicts has been limited to a few patients, but I found it unnecessary to modify my usual psychoanalytic approach. As in my earlier experiences investigating psychotic conditions like schizophrenia … I feel that progress in understanding the specific psychopathology of addiction must come through the understanding of transference neurosis or transference psychosis (p. 129).

Bion's comments in some places would seem to be elliptical, while in other places there are some clear assertions which make immediate sense, for instance:

> It is necessary not so at least there is one person, the analyst, who knows what he is doing. The analysand uses the analyst in the same way he uses the drug, that is, he treats him as an inanimate object (p. 129).

Elsewhere Bion appears to add to Rosenfeld's ideas, for instance in the section where Rosenfeld talks about psychic defence, Bion adds: "The psychiatrist and the environment also put great stress on the patient and compel him to cure himself with drugs in sheer self defence" (p. 128). It would seem to be a notable provocative aside; is Bion portraying the prescribing psychiatrist as a villain of the professional piece and that the patient is compelled to take drugs to find some cure from the psychiatrist? Bion here might be anticipating what we now think of as the self-medication principle (Khantzian & Albanese, 2008), that is to say many addicts use drugs in an attempt to medicate themselves against an underlying mental health problem.

In other notes Bion critiques Rosenfeld's theory and direction of interpretations and, commenting on one case where the patient appears to punish himself with his repetitious destructivity, Bion offers another angle: "The punishment and the identification are both substitutes for the depression" (p. 131). This may seem a minor observation, but it should be loudly applauded. There is one comment in particular in which Bion offers a neat summing up of his response to Rosenfeld, setting us off on a potentially new trajectory:

> I suspect drug addiction falls into the class in which all symptoms are cornered in one object by way of control. It is the same class as stammer, hypochondria. It might be called concentration for annihilation just as the constant conjunction could be concentration for creative purposes. Drug addiction is itself an example of precocious concentration which has to be broken into its component parts. Anyone who is prepared to annihilate a part of his personality is liable to annihilate all of it (p. 128).

The concept of "concentration for annihilation" is intriguing. The idea that sustained substance misuse annihilates more and more parts of the personality would seem to make sense; the self is attacked until in the end there is nothing left, the personality is vacated. I am not sure that I would necessarily concur with the comparison of drug misuse with stammering, but like Rosenfeld, Bion appears to be looking for shared psychological states, such as hypochondria, with which to anchor the impression of drug addiction. What Bion means about precocious concentration is worth elaborating too, and I will say more about this later. But before I do that I want to examine how Bion carried forward some of these speculations on Rosenfeld, especially in his book *Second Thoughts* (1967) where he develops his ideas about drug misuse.

Concentration for annihilation—creating the psychotic vacuum

As Rosenfeld (1960, 1965) had seen features of addiction that could be compared to other psychotic states such as chronic and acute schizophrenia and hypochondria, so Bion (1967) was inclined to compare the clinical presentation of addiction and psychosis. Just as Rosenfeld saw the drug being used as an idealized object which could reinforce hallucinated states as a defence against reality, Bion likewise saw drug use as a response to what he called a "hatred of reality". In other words a psychotic retreat was preferred to an experience of real life. In the chapter in *Second Thoughts* titled "Notes on the Theory of Schizophrenia", Bion tells us that he arrived at his formulation about psychotic processes based on his work with six patients:

three schizophrenics, two drug users, and one patient with obsessional anxiety. We see straight away that Bion compresses these three separate presentations into a theoretical whole, which in itself is notable. There is one case in particular which stands out for attention and illustrates what we might think of as psychotic repetition-compulsion, or psychotic fixation. The case is this. Bion notices a patient has been adopting a peculiar behaviour whereby on entering the consulting room he looks at Bion and then, as he lowers himself onto the couch, he fixes his gaze into one particular corner of the room. This ritual has probably been going on for some time, Bion surmises, and he admits that he had almost been half-asleep to it:

> I hardly know when I began to notice. ... The pattern must have often been there, though overlaid, as it seemed to me at the time, by other features that required more urgent interpretation. The gradual obtrusion, through constant repetition, of a pattern of behaviour which, when I recognised it, seemed already to be familiar, was a common experience with this patient (1967, p. 66).

He realizes that this habit had been commonplace, but the therapy had progressed reasonably enough. However, the patient was prone to lapsing into a silent impasse predicated by him saying: "I feel empty, I can do no more today." As Bion begins to understand the meaning of the ritual of gazing into the corner of the room, he sees that it is a repeating concentration that effectively serves as a defensive manoeuvre. Bion surmised that the client, after entering the room and internalizing him with an initial gaze, then goes on to evacuate him into the corner of the room. Thus Bion felt that the repetitive fixed gaze into the corner meant that the initial connection between him and the patient could only be short-lived and that the link was severed and the intimacy neutralized. Thus, having concentrated to annihilate Bion, the patient was left feeling empty: "I feel empty", and so the session would dip into a silent impasse. A vacuum was created where a connection had been.

Bion also noted this type of defensive manoeuvre in other cases where psychosis featured, referring to the hatred of reality leading to an exchange where what he calls schizophrenic ecstasy with utopian delusions, for instance of world domination, might be installed. In an idea that paralleled Rosenfeld, Bion referred to psychotic hallucinations as "unburdening the psyche" (1965, p. 83). The unburdened psyche is a landscape that is at once emptied out, perhaps an apocalyptic space. It is a thread of devastation or nameless dread that runs through Bion's thinking, and we can date it back to his experience of the horrors he endured in the First World War (Bion, 1992). We might surmise then that alleviation from addiction and psychosis, or recovery if you like, involves working through a devastating depression and the sense of vacuum that exist between the client and others. As Bion notes in his margin comment in Rosenfeld's book, this concentrated annihilation of the personality is the destructive counterpart to the potential for healthy concentration towards creativity.

This idea of a concentrated focus of annihilation seems essential. I have explored this sense of repetition-compulsion, proposing a new object-relations schema which I have referred to as the "Prometheus Syndrome". Bion's idea of concentration suggests that the self-destructive attacks may not in the first place be directed at the whole self, but rather the whole self may be endangered as a consequence of the initial focused attacks.

Lucy

I want finally to develop the idea of the threat of annihilation with an idea which I refer to as "psychotic vacuum". In trying to draw together the preceding ideas about space and annihilation, I want to present some reflections on my work with one of my former clients where some of these dynamic features were extant in her presentation.

Between 1989 and 1994, I came to know Lucy Cameron, both during her time as an inpatient, then as an outpatient and during her follow-up. After she had moved on, she continued to correspond with me over the next twelve years or so, until the end of her life. In 2009 Lucy's sisters contacted me with the sad news that Lucy had died in November 2006 of mouth cancer at the age of 48. Lucy's sisters Emma and Julia wanted me to know that they and some friends were publishing a posthumous collection of Lucy's poems and drawings (Cameron, 2009). They thought that I might be interested to know that Lucy had dedicated a poem to me, and would I want to receive a copy of the book? In publishing the poems they wanted to pay tribute to Lucy, but they also hoped that the poems would be helpful to others who might also be struggling with addiction, or would be illuminating for people working with substance misusers. In the same spirit they gave me permission to write about Lucy and quote from her poems.

Lucy was a prolific writer, a bright and talented artist and musician; she was funny, clever, and tragic in shared proportions. She had played the saxophone with various groups, and with one of them she had been contracted to record so her playing had made it onto vinyl. But she was a woman fraught with troubles. While using drugs, Lucy would appear to be more coherent, albeit in a manner perhaps described as cold and calculating, more out of desperation rather than confidence I would say. But to some extent her using self was more organized compared to the occasions when she had ceased drugs. Her warmth and humanity were apparent when she ceased, but she would be more unravelled and vulnerable, perhaps closer to her true self. Drugs were a sort of self-medication for her: she appeared to fit the self-medication hypothesis (Khantzian & Albanese, 2008), that is to say, drugs were fending off the anxieties and depression that surfaced when she was not using. I saw her undergo three withdrawals. Each time, at first she would become thought disordered, chaotic, and confused, sometimes suffering hallucinations and delusions. And then later she would experience crippling anxieties and phobias. It was a no-win situation; on the one hand she needed drugs to prop her up, but in using them she would became terribly physically deteriorated, her injecting habits and drinking leading to an endless train of illnesses.

I first met Lucy in 1989. Over the next five years I worked with her both as an inpatient and as an outpatient. And during the next twelve years or so, until near the end of her life, she stayed in touch, writing often, and occasionally we spoke on the telephone. Her letters were sometimes typed, on other occasions handwritten; sometimes they were coherent, other times wild, jagged, and confusing. They were often darkly funny and ironic. She used the letters to tell her ongoing painful story. For my part I continued to write letters of referral, putting her in touch with colleagues depending on where she was, sometimes offering counsel.

It seemed to me that Lucy suffered from a spatial condition which Henri Rey has described as claustroagorophia (Rey, 1994). Lucy could not be inside because she felt trapped and panicky, but she could not be outside because she felt cut adrift and alone. Her detoxifications were torturous: she would see blood-filled baths, or the walls would be cracking, or people would be coming through the walls to get her.

Moving in and out of rooms for her was like crossing thresholds of terror. When she was clean and sober she seemed to move through the world as if she were cowering, as if something were about to drop onto to her. There was no space that felt comfortable for Lucy and she seemed to spend much of her life in a nomadic search for a secure base. I remember in one session shortly after she had completed her detoxification from opiates that she told me that I shouldn't talk to her: "My breath is like death," and she said if I talked to her I too would die. She said everyone around her died. Indeed, several of her drug-using acquaintances had died, two in her presence. I did sometimes have an eerie sense that I did not want to talk to her, as if something terrible would happen. But I stayed with her as best I could; as one of my supervisors Jonathan Pedder would say: "Sometimes just hold onto your chair." Perhaps the worst loss that haunted Lucy was that her mother had died too soon. Although Lucy was 25 at the time, it seemed that she had never been able to get close to her mother. As a parent her mother was distant and remote. Lucy said that her mother had campaigned to save the world, but couldn't save herself. There was a sense that Lucy was looking for the safe haven of a mother.

Lucy had a preoccupation with the idea of a holey (sic) ghost. She would make drawings, and had an image of a skull tattooed onto her arm with the words "holey ghost" written underneath. In other words Lucy's ghost was a ghost with holes or spaces. It was a sort of double absence, if you like. It was hard to put this sense of void into words, but I always felt this inner emptiness was at Lucy's core. She tried desperately to find the words to describe these feelings in therapy; she doodled, painted, drew, and wrote in an effort to convey what she felt. In the end her poems probably struck closest to her meaning, as she compressed words and ideas. For instance in *Surrender* she talked about a "frightmare zoocage". One reviewer of her poems (Russell, 2010) was particularly taken with the poem *Crossword Puzzles* which he said was a:

> clever play on that stock term: cross words are angry words; angry words cause confusion and misunderstanding. The partner in question is a crossword addict, and Lucy in the role of a "crossword widow". She associates crosswords with cold macho logic, finds them lacking in both spirit and humour. She longs for an astronaut, who could travel with her in zero gravity … and blow

multicoloured bubbles out of his ample arse. She could also relish a spider, appreciation of the aesthetics of a straight line in one thread of a web, and one who "has his webs well hung" (double entendre reference to lack of passion in her partner?) (Russell, 2010).

Perhaps Lucy's saxophone playing was also an attempt to converse, to express how she was feeling. Her holey ghost drawings seemed to show something of her frenzied state of mind: a skeletal frame, a body-mind wasted by substances, ravaged by lack of good food for thought. The holey ghost tattoo on her arm imprinted her state of living death, as if she was alive and dead at the same, there and not there simultaneously. There was a void that seemed to suck life out of her. As Bion described, the concentration to annihilation for Lucy in the end outdid her creative life force. The abiding tone of the poems is the painful sense of hanging on, relationships crash into each other, and are torn apart in agony. I remember the occasion she left the inpatient unit in 1991 when Lucy asked if she could hug me, to which I unusually agreed. We hugged briefly, but as we separated one of her long dangly earrings caught on my jumper. I remember the jumper well because it was one that my Nanna had knitted me (a multi-coloured punky jumper; I had picked the wool). It seemed to take an eternity for Lucy to detach her earring. To some extent our separation was never satisfactorily completed.

Lucy's death at the age of 48 had the familiar sense of untimeliness that has been a recurring feature of working with addicted clients. Of all of the work I have been engaged in over the last thirty years of acute psychiatry and mental health, I have seen more casualties who have been addicts than any other clinical condition. Death becomes the space too often, and we still have very limited resources and theories about addiction. I want to finish with one of Lucy's poems called *The Space*, which I think gives us some sense of the vacuum that Lucy carried with her.

The space *(fragment)*

> This is the space where no one can reach you
> Nothing can touch you
> This is the space where you're down on your knees
> Begging blindly please for a reason to restart

This is the silence of people kept apart
This is the space where there's nothing nowhere
There's nothing in here, no one out there
Nothing to make you want to stay
No one to take you away
This is the space where silence aches in your brain
And emptiness is a physical pain
This is the space, your eternal allotted place.

The poem is important not just because it tells us of the sense of isolation for Lucy, but also because it speaks to us of the loneliness that is at the very heart of all mental distress. From this we can learn.

REFERENCES

Abraham, H. C. (1974). Karl Abraham: an unfinished biography. *International Review of Psycho-Analysis*, 1: 17–72.

Abraham, K. (1913). *Dreams and Myths. A Study in Race Psychology*. New York: The Journal of Nervous and Mental Disease Publishing Co.

Abraham, K. (1927). *Selected Papers of Karl Abraham*. London: Hogarth and Institute of Psychoanalysis.

Anonymous (1971). *Go Ask Alice*. London: Corgi, 1982.

Balint, M. (1968). *The Basic Fault*. London: Tavistock.

Barham, M. (1992). *Closing the Asylum*. Harmondsworth: Penguin.

Barnes, M. & Berke, J. (1971). *Mary Barnes: Two Accounts of a Journey Through Madness (with Mary Barnes)*. London: MacGibbon & Kee.

Barrie, J. M. (1928). *My Lady Nicotine*. London: Hodder & Stoughton.

Bennett, G. A., Velleman, R. D., Barter, G. & Bradbury, C. (2000). Gender differences in sharing injecting equipment by drug users in England. *Aids Care*, 12(1): 77–87.

Berke, J. (2009). *Malice Through the Looking Glass. Reflections and Refractions of Envy, Greed and Jealousy*. London: Teva.

Berke, J. (2010). Some considerations of the therapeutic potential of regression. *Psychosis*, 1(4):1–7 .

Berke, J., Fagan, M., Mak-Pearce, G. & Pierides-Muller, S. (Eds.) (2001). *Beyond Madness: Psychosocial Interventions in Psychosis*. London: Jessica Kingsley.

113

Bernfeld, S. & Feitelberg, S. (1931). The principle of entropy & the death instinct. *International Journal of Psychoanalysis, 12*: 61–81.

Bion, W. R. (1967). *Second Thoughts*. London: Maresfield.

Bion, W. R. (1970). *Transformations*. London. Maresfield.

Bion, W. R. (1975). *A Memoir of the Future. Book One: The Dream*. Rio de Janeiro, Brazil: Imago Editora.

Bion, W. R. (1975). Memoir of a Future. London: Karnac, 1990.

Bion, W. R. (1997). *War Memoirs 1917–1919*. London: Karnac.

Bomford, A. (1998). Personal communication.

Bowers, L., Brennan, G., Winship, G. & Theodoridou, C. (2010). *Acutely Psychotic People: Communication Skills for Nurses and Professionals Working with People Who are Very Mentally Ill*. [Monograph.] London: City University.

Breton, A. & Soupault, A. (1920). *Magnetic Fields*. London, Atlas, 1985.

Burroughs, W. (1959). *Naked Lunch*. Paris: Olympia.

Cameron, L. (2009). *Rubbish Up the Messheads*. London: Squiffy.

Campbell, J. (1959). *The Masks of God—Primitive Mythology*. London: Souvenir.

Cocteau, J. (1930). *Opium*. London: Peter Owen, 1968.

Connell, P. H. (1968). The use and abuse of amphetamines. *The Practitioner, 200*: 234–243.

Cottle, J. (1847). *Reminiscences of Samuel Taylor Coleridge & Robert Southey*. London: Basil Savage, 1970.

Dawe, S., Powell, J., Richards, D., Gossop, M., Marks, I., Strang, J. & Gray, J. (1993). Does post-withdrawal cue exposure improve outcome in opiate addiction treatment? *Addiction, 88*: 1233–1245.

De Quincey, T. (1907). *Confessions of an English Opium Eater*. London: J. M. Dent, 1930.

De Wet, C. J., Reed, L. J. & Bearn, J. (2005). The rise of buprenorphine prescribing in England: analysis of NHS regional data, 2001–2003. *Addiction, 100*(4): 495–499.

Durkheim, E. (1952). *Suicide. A Study in Sociology*. London: Routledge & Kegan Paul.

English, C. (2011). Object relations & drug-addiction. [PhD thesis.] University of Nottingham.

Fairbairn, W. R. D. (1930). Libido theory re-evaluated. In: *Instinct to Self. Volume II*. Northvale, NJ: Jason Aronson, 1994.

Farson, D. (1975). *The Man Who Wrote Dracula. A Biography of Bram Stoker*. London: Michael Joseph.

Fenichel, O. (1945). Drug addiction. In: *The Psychoanalytic Theory of Neurosis* (pp. 377–379]. New York: Guilford Press.

Frazer, J. G. (1922). *The Golden Bough—A Study in Magic and Religion*. New York: Macmillan.

Freud, S. (1900a). *The Interpretation of Dreams. S. E., 5*. London: Hogarth.

Freud, S. (1905d). Three essays on the theory of sexuality. *S. E., 7*. London: Hogarth.

Freud, S. (1913). *Totem and Taboo. S. E., 13*. London: Routledge & Kegan Paul, 1950.

Freud, S. (1917e). *Mourning and Melancholia. S. E., 14*: 243–258. London: Hogarth.

Freud, S. (1920g). Beyond the pleasure principle. *S. E., 18*. London: Hogarth.

Freud, S. (1924). The economic problem of masochism. *S. E., 19*: 155–172. London: Hogarth.

Freud, S. (1930a). *Civilization and its Discontents. S. E., 21*. London: Hogarth.

Freud, S. (1932). On the control of fire. *Collected Papers. Vol V.* London: Hogarth, 1957.

Freud, S. (1940). *An Outline of Psychoanalysis*. London: Hogarth.

Freud, S. & Abraham, K. (1965). *A Psycho-Analytic Dialogue. The Letters of Sigmund Freud and Karl Abraham 1907–1926*. London: Hogarth and Institute of Psychoanalysis.

Glover, E. (1932). On the aetiology of drug addiction. *International Journal of Psychoanalysis, 13*: 298–328.

Godfrey, C., Stewart, D. & Gossop, M. (2004). Economic analysis of costs and consequences of the treatment of drug misuse: 2-year outcome data from the National Treatment Outcome Research Study (NTORS). *Addiction, 99*(6): 697–707.

Gossop, M. (1982). *Living With Drugs*. London: Temple Smith.

Hinshelwood, R. D. (2001). *Thinking about Institutions. Mileux and Madness*. London: Jessica Kingsley.

Hopper, E. (1995). A psychoanalytic theory of "drug addiction". *International Journal of Psychoanalysis, 76*: 1121–1142.

Horowitz, I. L. (1957). *War & Peace in Contemporary Social & Philosophical Theory*. London: *Souvenir Press*, 1973.

Hunter, G. M., Stimson, G. V., Judd, A., Jones, S. & Hickman, M. (2000). Measuring injecting risk behaviour in the second decade of harm reduction: a survey of injecting drug users in England. *Addiction, 95*(9): 1351–1361.

Illich, I. (1976). *Limits of Medicine*. Harmondsworth: Penguin, 1990.

Jackson, M. (2001). *Weathering the Storms: Psychotherapy for Psychosis*. London: Karnac.

Jackson, M. (2002). Henri Rey. http://www.melanie-klein-trust.org.uk/rey2002.htm. Accessed 3.3.2010.

Jackson, M. & Williams, P. (1994). *Unimaginable Storms*. London: Karnac.

Joseph, B. (1982). Addiction to near death. *International Journal of Psychoanalysis, 63*: 449–456.

Kaufman, E. (1991). Critical aspects of the psychodynamics of substance abuse and the evaluation of their application to a psychotherapeutic approach. *The International Journal of Addictions, 25*(2): 97–116.

Kerenyi, C. (1977). *Dionysus—Archetypal Images of Indestructible Life*. Princeton, NJ: Princeton University Press.

Kerouac, J. (1958). *The Subterraneans*. New York: Grove.

Khantzian, E. & Albanese, M. J. (2008). *Addiction as Self Medication*. Lanham, MD: Rowman & Littlefield.

Klein, M. (1946). Notes on some schizoid mechanisms. In: *Envy and Gratitude and Other Works 1946–1963* [pp. 1–24]. London: Virago, 1988.

Klein, M. (1948). *Contributions to Psychoanalysis 1921–1945*. London: Hogarth.

Klein, M. (1963). The Oresteia. In: *Envy and Gratitude and Other Works 1946–1963* [pp. 275–299]. London: Virago, 1988.

Klein, M. (1988). *Love, Guilt and Reparation and Other Works 1921–1945*. London: Virago.

Kohut, H. (1971). *The Analysis of the Self*. New York: New York University Press.

Kohut, H. (1977). *The Restoration of the Self*. New York: New York University Press.

Laing, A. C. (1994). *R. D. Laing: A Biography*. London: Peter Owen.

Lasch, C. (1979). *The Culture of Narcissism. American Life in an Age of Diminishing Expectations*. London: W. W. Norton.

Leary, T. (1970). *The Politics of Ecstasy*. London: Paladin.

Leatherdale, C. (1985). *Dracula. The Novel and the Legend*. Wellingborough, UK: Aquarian.

Leatherdale, C. (1987). *The Origins of Dracula*. London: William Kimber.

Lefebure, M. (1977). *Samuel Taylor Coleridge: a Bondage of Opium*. New York: Quartet.

Lévi-Strauss, C. (1963). *Structural Anthropology*. Harmondsworth: Penguin, 1993.

Limentani, A. (1986). On the psychodynamics of drug dependence. In: *Between Freud and Klein* [pp. 48–65]. London: Free Association.

Low, B. (1920). *Psycho-Analysis*. New York: Harcourt, Brace & Howe.

Lucas, R. (1993). The Psychotic Wavelength. *Psychoanalytic Psychotherapy, 7*(1): 15–24.

Lucas, R. (2009). *The Psychotic Wavelength*. London: Routledge.

Ludlam, H. (1962). *A Biography of Dracula*. The Life Story of Bram Stoker. Slough, UK: W. Foulsham.

MacDonald, S., Newrith, C., Blyth, F. & Winship, G. (1998). Adolescent transition and the use of hallucinogens. *British Journal of Psychotherapy, 15*(2): 240–248.

Marcuse, H. (1964). *One Dimensional Man*. Boston: Beacon Press.

Marcuse, H. (1968). *Essay on Liberation*. Harmondsworth: Penguin, 1969.

Marlatt, G. A. & Gordon, J. R. (1985). *Relapse Prevention: Maintenance Strategies in the Treatment of Addictive Behaviour*. New York: Guilford Press.

Mitchell, S. A. (1994). Recent developments in psychoanalytic theorizing. *Journal of Psychotherapy Integration, 4*(2): 93–103.

Mueser, K. & Lewis, S. (2000). Treatment of substance misuse in schizophrenia. In: P. F. Buckley & J. L. Waddington (Eds.), *Schizophrenia and Mood Disorders—the New Drug Therapies in Clinical Practice* [pp. 286–296]. London: Butterworth Heinemann.

Pater, W. (1895). *Greek Studies*. London: Macmillan, 1904.

Pedder, J. R. (2010). Fear of dependency in therapeutic relationships. In: G. Winship (Ed. and commentary), *From Attachment to New Beginnings in Psychoanalytic Therapy*. London: Karnac.

Pines, M. (1984). Reflections on mirroring. *International Review of Psycho-Analysis, 11*: 27–42.

Pines, M. (1985). Mirroring and child development. *Psychoanalytic Enquiry, 5*(2): 211–231.

Plant, S. (1999). *Writing on Drugs*. London: Faber & Faber.

Powell, J., Dawe, S., Richards, D., Gossop, M., Marks, I., Strang, J. & Gray, J. (1993). Can opiate addicts tell us about their relapse risk? Subjective predictors of clinical prognosis. *Addictive Behaviours, 18*: 473–490.

Rado, S. (1926). The psychic effects of intoxicants. *International Journal of Psychoanalysis, 7*: 396–413.

Reuter, P. & Pollack, H. (2006). How much can treatment reduce national drug problems? *Addiction, 101*(3): 341–347.

Rey, H. (1994a). Further thoughts on "that which patients bring to analysis". *British Journal of Psychotherapy, 11*(2): 185–197.

Rey, H. (1994b). Further thoughts on "that which patients bring to analysis". *British Journal of Psychotherapy, 11*(2): 185–197.

Rosenfeld, D. (1992). *The Psychotic Aspects of the Personality*. London: Karnac.

Rosenfeld, H. (1960). On drug addiction. *International Journal of Psychoanalysis, 41*: 467–475.

Rosenfeld, H. (1965). *Psychotic States*. London: Hogarth.

Russell, D. (2010). Rubbish up the messheads, by Lucy Cameron. [Book Review.] *Poetry Express, 32*: 30–32. http://www.survivorspoetry.com/pages/poetry-express.php. Accessed July 2010.

Rustin, M. (2001). *Reason & Unreason*. London: Continuum.

Sandler, J. (1988). *Projection, Identification and Projective Identification*. London: Karnac.

Schoor, E. V. (1992). Pathological narcissism and addiction. *Psychoanalytic Psychotherapy, 6*(3): 205–211.

Shelley, P. (1820). *Prometheus Unbound*. In: *Collected Works*. Oxford: Oxford University Press, 1988.

Shengold, L. (1991). *Father Can't You See I'm Burning*. New Haven, CT: Yale University Press.

Smith, H. M., Alexander, G. J. M., Webb, G., McManus, T., McFarlane, T. G. & Williams, R. (1992). Hepatitis B and delta virus infection among "at risk" populations in South East London. *Journal of Epidemiology and Community Health, 46*(2): 144–147.

Steiner, J. (1993). *Psychic Retreats*. London: Routledge.

Steiner, J. (1995). The influence of Henri Rey's work. *Psychoanalytic Psychotherapy, 9*(2): 145–148.

Stevenson, R. L. (1886). *Strange Case of Dr Jekyll and Mr Hyde*. New York: Charles Scribner's Sons.

Stoker, B. (1897). *Dracula*. Oxford: Oxford University Press.

Strang, J. (1982). Psychotherapy by nurses—some special characteristics. *Journal of Advanced Nursing, 7*: 167–171.

Szasz, T. (1974). *Ceremonial Chemistry. The Ritual Persecution of Drugs, Addicts & Pushers*. London: Routledge & Kegan Paul, 1975.

Winnicott, D. W. (1971). *Playing and Reality*. London: Tavistock.

Winship, G. (1999). Addiction, death and the liver in mind: the Prometheus Syndrome. *Psychoanalytic Psychotherapy, 13*(1): 41–49.

Winship, G. (2007). The ethics of reflective research in single case study inquiry. *Perspective in Psychiatric Care, 43*(4): 174–182.

Winship, G. & Hardy, S. (2007). Perspectives on the prevalence and treatment of personality disorder. *Journal of Psychiatric and Mental Health Nursing, 14*(2): 148–154.

Winship, G. & Unwin, C. (1997). Psychotherapy and nursing interventions. In: H. Rassool & M. Guffor (Eds.), *Addiction Nursing*. Cheltenham: Nelson Thornes.

Wurmser, L. (1974). Psychoanalytic considerations of the etiology of compulsive drug use. *Journal of the American Psychoanalytical Association, 22*: 820–843.

INDEX